BOOK
2

Expressions

Meaningful English Communication

David Nunan

HEINLE & HEINLE

TM

THOMSON LEARNING

Australia · Canada · Mexico · Singapore · Spain · United Kingdom · United States

HEINLE & HEINLE

TM

THOMSON LEARNING

Editorial Director: Nancy Leonhardt
Production Director: Elise Kaiser
Editorial Manager: Christopher Wenger
Senior Development Editor: Sean Bermingham
Development Editor: Colin Toms
Production Editor: Tan Jin Hock

Senior Marketing Manager: Amy Mabley
Interior/Cover Design: Christopher Hanzie, TYA Inc.
Illustrations: Raketshop Design Studio, Philippines
Cover Images: Photodisc
Composition: TYA Inc.
Printer: Seng Lee Press

For more information, contact Heinle & Heinle Publishers, 20 Park Plaza, Boston, MA 02116 USA. Or you can visit our Internet site at http://www.heinle.com

UK/EUROPE/MIDDLE EAST:
Thomson Learning
Berkshire House
168-173 High Holborn
London WC1V 7AA
United Kingdom

CANADA:
Nelson/Thomson Learning
1120 Birchmount Road
Toronto, Ontario
Canada M1K 5G4

ASIA (including India):
Thomson Learning
60 Albert Street
#15-01 Albert Complex
Singapore 189969

AUSTRALIA/NEW ZEALAND:
Nelson/Thomson Learning
102 Dodds Street
South Melbourne
Victoria 3205, Australia

LATIN AMERICA:
Thomson Learning
Seneca 53
Colonia Polanco
11560 México, D.F. México

SPAIN:
Paraninfo/Thomson Learning
Calle Magallanes 25
28105 Madrid
Espana

For permission to use the material from this text or product, contact us in the US by
Tel 1 (800) 730-2214
Fax 1 (800) 730-2215
www.thomsonrights.com

Every effort has been made to trace all sources of illustrations/photos/information in this book, but if any have been inadvertently overlooked, the publisher will be pleased to make the necessary arrangements at the first opportunity.

ISBN 0-8384-2245-4

Printed in Singapore
1 2 3 4 5 6 04 03 02 01 00

AUTHOR'S ACKNOWLEDGMENTS

As always, in a project of this magnitude, there are many people to thank. First and foremost, I would like to acknowledge and thank Christopher Wenger, ELT Editorial Manager for Asia at Heinle & Heinle/Thomson Learning. It was Chris who first saw the potential of *Expressions* and did more than anyone to bring it to fruition. To Grace Low for her contributions to the Read On sections. To John Chapman for his workbooks. To Colin Toms for his detailed and insightful editing. To Nancy Leonhardt for her faith in this project and in me. To Christopher Hanzie, Stella Tan and the staff at T.Y.A. for their round-the-clock efforts under nearly impossible deadlines.

I am indebted to numerous other folks within Heinle & Heinle: Amy Mabley, John Lowe, Ian Martin, Francisco Lozano, Carmelita Benozatti, Sean Bermingham and Tan Jin Hock who, as always, are a joy to work with. I can't thank you enough for your support.

In addition to the above, I would like to extend my thanks to the following professionals who have offered invaluable comments and suggestions during the development of the series:

• Esperanza Bañuelos	CECATI, Mexico City, Mexico
• Graham Bathgate	ELEC, Tokyo, Japan
• James Boyd	ECC Foreign Language Institute, Osaka, Japan
• Gunther Breaux	Dongduk Women's University, Seoul, Korea
• Robert Burgess	NAVA Language Schools, Bangkok, Thailand
• Connie Chang	ELSI, Taipei, Taiwan
• Clara Inés García Frade	Universidad Militar 'Nueva Granada,' Santafé de Bogotá, Colombia
• Rob Gorton	Kumamoto YMCA, Kumamoto, Japan
• Randall Grev	ELSI, Taipei, Taiwan
• Ross Hackshaw	IAI Girls' Junior & Senior High School, Hakodate, Japan
• Ann-Marie Hadzima	National Taiwan University, Taipei, Taiwan
• Gladys Hong	The Overseas Chinese Institute of Technology, Taichung, Taiwan
• Ching-huei Huang	Oriental Institute of Technology, Taipei, Taiwan
• Ivon Katz	Asian University of Science & Technology, Chonburi, Thailand
• Tim Kirk	Asian University of Science & Technology, Chonburi, Thailand
• Clarice Lamb	ATLAS English Learning Centre, Porto Alegre, Brazil
• Lee Bal-geum	Seul-gi Young-o, Seoul, Korea
• Mike Lee	ELSI, Taipei, Taiwan
• Susan Lee	Seul-gi Young-o, Seoul, Korea
• Jisun Leigh	Hankook English Institute, Seoul, Korea
• Hsin-ying Li	National Taiwan University, Taipei, Taiwan
• Ian Nakamura	Hiroshima Kokusai Gakuin University, Hiroshima, Japan
• Luis Pantoja	Colegie Particular Andino, Huancayo, Peru
• Juan Ramiro Peña	Preparatoria - Benemérita Universidad, Autónoma de Puebla, Puebla, Mexico
• Susanna Philiproussis	Miyazaki International College, Kano, Japan
• P. Robin Rigby	Hakodate Shirayuri Gakuen Chugakko, Hakodate, Japan
• Lesley D. Riley	Kanazawa Institute of Technology, Ishikawa, Japan
• Mercedes Rossetti	Inglés en Línea S.A., Buenos Aires, Argentina
• Fortino Salazar	Instituto Benjamin Franklin, Mexico City, Mexico
• Beatriz Solina	ARICANA, Rosario, Argentina
• Carolyn Teh	ELSI, Kuala Lumpur, Malaysia
• Daisy William	ELSI, Kuala Lumpur, Malaysia

Scope and sequence

UNIT	Title	Goals	Structures	Listening
1 Page 8	Can I have your name, please?	• Stating intention/desire • Asking for and giving personal information	• Polite questions using *Can*	• Names and addresses
2 Page 16	I have two older sisters.	• Asking about family • Identifying family members	• Questions with *How many*	• Family photos
3 Page 24	What are you doing over the break?	• Asking about plans • Asking for specific information	• Present continuous for future	• Vacation plans
4 Page 32	Where did you go on vacation?	• Asking and talking about vacation activities	• Questions and statements using simple past	• Vacation activities
5 Page 40	Can I help you?	• Asking about prices • Paying for items	• Quantifiers	• Shopping and prices
6 Page 48	What do do you?	• Describing occupations • Talking about likes and dislikes	• *Like* + ___*ing* and *get to* + verb	• Jobs and workplaces
7 Page 56	Could you do me a favor?	• Making requests • Thanking people	• *Need* and *need to*	• Phrases for requesting help
8 Page 64	Are you looking forward to your trip?	• Asking about plans • Expressing obligation • Making reservations	• *Have to* and *should*	• Travel options and reservations
9 Page 72	Turn left on Denver Street.	• Offering help • Asking for and giving directions	• Prepositions of location	• Map reading
10 Page 80	I drink too much coffee.	• Discussing personal habits • Talking about degrees	• *How much/how many/how often* and *too/enough*	• Personal habits
11 Page 88	Did you hear about Laura?	• Talking about past events • Expressing surprise • Offering congratulations	• *Get* + participle and *get* + noun phrase	• Congratulations and surprise
12 Page 96	I have a terrible headache.	• Discussing people's conditions • Giving advice	• *Should* and *much/a lot*	• Health problems and remedies
13 Page 104	Do you have any experience?	• Discussing job experience and education • Making comparisons	• *More/most* and *better/best*	• Job interviews
14 Page 112	Have you been to the new mall?	• Making plans • Discussing experience • Describing places	• *Have been*	• Past experiences
15 Page 120	I took your advice.	• Making recommendations • Describing places and objects	• *Why* and *because*	• Recommendations and reasons
16 Page 128	Did you mail those letters?	• Discussing errands • Apologizing • Making excuses	• *Was able to* and *had to*	• Errands and excuses

Pronunciation	Writing	Reading	Recycling
• Pronouncing *you* and *your*	• Applying to join a club	• Join our club! • *Skimming*	• Asking who people are • *Can*
• Word stress in replies	• Writing a letter to a host family	• Family reunions • *Scanning*	• Asking about families • *How many*
• Reduced *going to*	• Describing vacation plans	• Young people with a heart • *Inferring vocabulary*	• Asking for additional information • Present continuous verbs
• Rising and falling question intonation	• Writing a postcard	• Active vacations • *Scanning*	• *Wh-* questions • Talking about what you did
• Reduced sounds in prices	• Writing a recipe	• A world famous market • *Analyzing word parts*	• Numbers and prices • *Will have*
• Intonation to show attitude	• Describing your ideal job	• Inventions for the modern world • *Reviewing*	• Describing jobs • *Like*
• Reduced *could you* and *do you*	• Asking a favor	• A letter of thanks • *Reading actively*	• Questions with *Do you...?* • Offering and thanking
• Intonation in a series of items	• Writing for a travel brochure	• Accidental travelers • *Scanning*	• Making suggestions • Telling time
• Pronouncing numbers and addresses	• Giving directions	• Maps don't help here • *Identifying reference words*	• *Wh-* questions • Prepositions • Giving directions
• Sentence stress and rhythm patterns	• Writing a letter of advice	• How I broke a bad habit • *Inferring content*	• Describing routines • *How much/How many* • *Want to*
• Intonation to show surprise	• Writing a letter of congratulations	• Money isn't everything • *Inferring vocabulary*	• Past simple • Thanking people
• Reduced *and*	• Writing a get well card	• Environmental illness • *Identifying reference words*	• *Should* • Using degrees of description
• Syllable stress in words	• Writing a letter of application	• A new kind of summer job • *Scanning*	• Asking about past events • *Let's*
• Reduced *want to* and *want a*	• Writing an invitation email	• See Paris on wheels • *Scanning*	• Present continuous for future • Inviting
• Sentence stress and rhythm patterns	• Writing an ad for your hometown	• Advice through proverbs • *Inferring content*	• Making suggestions • Adverbs of degree
• Pronouncing contractions with *not*	• Writing a note of apology	• The right time • *Scanning*	• *Will* • Past simple • Making excuses

Useful Classroom Expressions

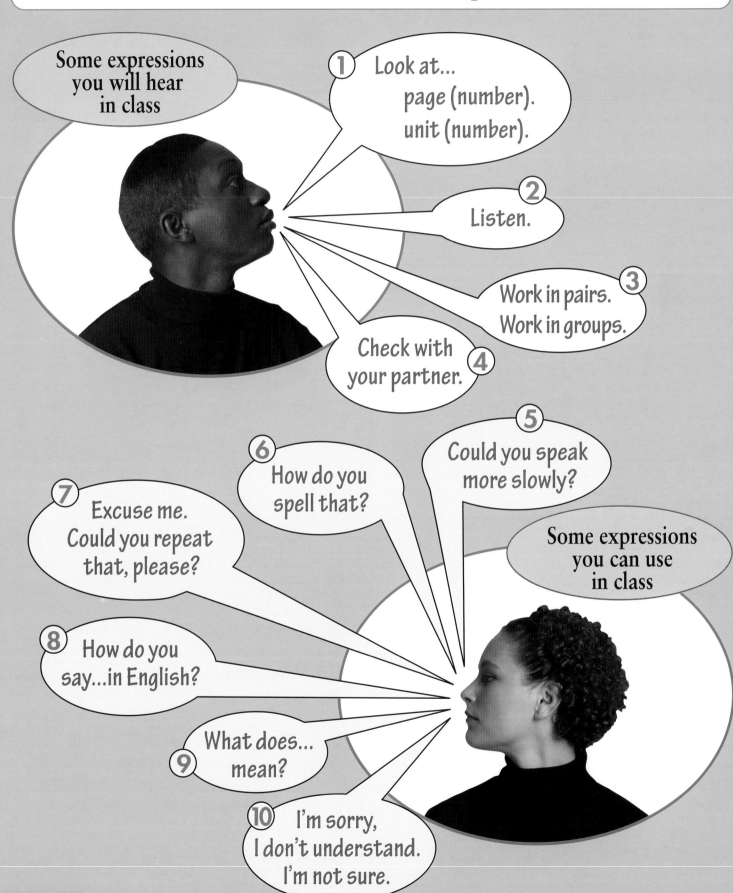

Some expressions you will hear in class

1 Look at...
   page (number).
   unit (number).

2 Listen.

3 Work in pairs.
   Work in groups.

4 Check with your partner.

Some expressions you can use in class

5 Could you speak more slowly?

6 How do you spell that?

7 Excuse me. Could you repeat that, please?

8 How do you say...in English?

9 What does... mean?

10 I'm sorry, I don't understand. I'm not sure.

How do you like to learn?

A) Preferences

○ Which do you like? Put these in order (1–6).

_____ Speaking _____ Reading _____ Grammar

_____ Listening _____ Writing _____ Vocabulary

B) In class, I like...

○ Check (✔) the boxes.

	Not at all	A little	A lot	Not sure
doing role plays				
playing language games				
listening to tapes				
watching videos				
doing pair work				
doing group work				
studying grammar				
listening to the teacher				
writing things down				

C) Out of class, I like...

○ Check (✔) the boxes.

	Not at all	A little	A lot	Not sure
talking with native English speakers				
watching English TV/movies				
reading English newspapers/books				
studying by myself				
writing letters/a diary in English				
doing homework				
studying from textbooks				
learning English from the Internet				

Check your ideas with a partner. Now you're ready to start *Expressions 2.*

Goals

⬤ *Stating intention/desire* ⬤ *Asking for and giving personal information*

Can I have your name, please?

1 Get Ready

A Write the number of each activity in the correct place in the picture.

1. hockey
2. drama
3. swimming
4. music
5. chess
6. tennis

B Can you think of any other types of clubs? List them.

Sports clubs	Other clubs
_____	_____
_____	_____
_____	_____

2 Start Talking

A Look at the conversation and listen.

Jenny: Can I help you?
John: Yes, please. I want to join the drama club.
Jenny: Sure. Can I have your name, please?
John: It's John Lemke.
Jenny: How do you spell that?
John: J-O-H-N L-E-M-K-E.

Pair work **B** Practice with a partner.
Then practice again using other clubs and different names.

3 Listen In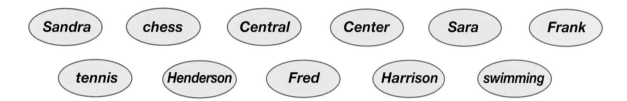

(A) **Look at the words below. Which are first names for men?**
Which are first names for women? Which are family names?

(Sandra)   (chess)   (Central)   (Center)   (Sara)   (Frank)

(tennis)   (Henderson)   (Fred)   (Harrison)   (swimming)

(B) **Listen and circle the words you hear.**

(C) **Listen again and complete the forms.**

First Name: _____
Last Name: *Graziani*
Address: _____
Tel. No.: *654-1073*
Club: _____

First Name: _____
Last Name: _____
Address: *3230 Harrison Street*
Tel. No.: _____
Club: *swimming*

Try this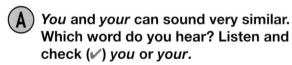

Which expression has the same meaning as *OK*? Can you remember?

4 Say It Right

(A) *You* and *your* can sound very similar. Which word do you hear? Listen and check (✔) *you* or *your*.

You	Your
1.	
2.	
3.	
4.	
5.	

(B) **Write two sentences with *you* and *your*.**

_____
_____
_____
_____

Pair work (C) **Say your sentences to your partner. Your partner will say *you* or *your*.**

5 Focus In

(A) Look at the chart.

Polite questions using *Can*	
What's your name?	It's Philip Hall.
Can you tell me your name, please?	
What's your address?	1013 Main Street.
Can I have your address, please?	
What's your telephone number?	711-2983.
Can you give me your telephone number, please?	

(B) Fill in the blanks. Then write the number of the question next to the correct answer.

1. ___Can___ you tell me your telephone number?   _____ At 315 Oak Street.
2. _____ your first name?   _____ Sure, it's 22 Neil Road, Hope.
3. Can I _____ your address, please?   _____ Yes, it's Emily Johnson.
4. Can _____ give me your full name, please?   _____ Kevin.
5. Excuse me. Where _____ you live?   _____ It's 276-8767.

(C) Read the questions. Write polite questions with *Can...?* that are similar in meaning.

1. Where do you live? _____
2. What's your family name? _____
3. What's your phone number? _____
4. What's your date of birth? _____

6 Talk Some More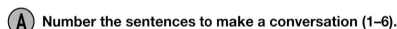

(A) Number the sentences to make a conversation (1–6).

Jenny: __1__ What's your address, John?

John: _____ 254 Summit Street.

John: _____ 278-7842.

John: __6__ Thanks.

Jenny: _____ OK. The first meeting will be tomorrow at 5:00 in Room 315. See you then.

Jenny: _____ All right. And your phone number?

(B) Check your answers.

Pair work

(C) Practice the conversation with a partner. Use your own information.

> **Spotlight**
> Instead of repeating the same question word, we can start the next question with *And...*

Work In Pairs — Student A

A Your partner wants to join the fencing club. Ask questions and fill in the form.

FENCING CLUB
Registration Form

Name _____

Address _____

_____

Telephone _____

How do you spell that?

B Join the hockey club using the information below.

THOMSON UNIVERSITY

Name: Bill Jennings

Address: 28 Walker Avenue

Telephone: 633-5480

Join the Thomson University
Hockey Club

Register Now!

C You and your partner want to join new clubs. Choose a club and give your details to your partner. Fill in your partner's details.

Club: _____

Name: _____

Tel. No.: _____

Address: _____

_____

Try this

Close your book. Now say your partner's information.
Your partner will check your information. Did you remember correctly?

Can I have your name, please?

Work In Pairs Student B

A Join the fencing club using the information below.

Join the Newton University
Fencing Club

Register Now!

NEWTON UNIVERSITY

Name: _Alison Gerber_

Address: _939 Farley Street_

Telephone: _835-1637_

B Your partner wants to join the hockey club. Ask questions and fill in the form.

How do you spell that?

HOCKEY CLUB
— Registration Form —

Name
_____

Address
_____
_____

Telephone
_____

C You and your partner want to join new clubs. Choose a club and give your details to your partner. Fill in your partner's details.

Club: _____
Name: _____
Tel. No.: _____
Address: _____
_____

Try this

Close your book. Now say your partner's information.
Your partner will check your information. Did you remember correctly?

Express Yourself

A Survey. Ask your classmates questions to find the information below. Write a different name for each. Note any information you find out under *Details*.

Find someone who...	Name	Details
1. lives close to you		
2. lives far from you		
3. has a cell phone number		
4. belongs to a club		

B Work in groups. What questions did you ask to get the answers in part A? Make a list. Compare your questions and answers.

 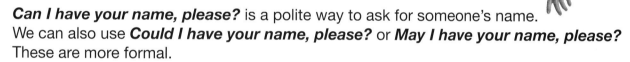 *Think About It*

Can I have your name, please? is a polite way to ask for someone's name. We can also use ***Could I have your name, please?*** or ***May I have your name, please?*** These are more formal.

• In what situations do you think you might hear them?

10 **Write About It**

A Look at the note.

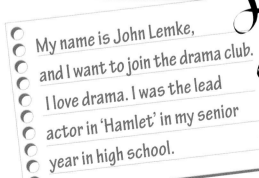

My name is John Lemke, and I want to join the drama club. I love drama. I was the lead actor in 'Hamlet' in my senior year in high school.

B Now write a note asking to join a university club. Say why you want to join and why you would be a good member.

Can I have your name, please? **13**

• **Strategy: Skimming**

Do you have extra time on your hands?

Join the International

Club Absolutely free!

Practice conversation
Learn slang
Write to keypals in other countries
and much more!
Every Thursday 5:00–6:00 p.m.
Email Donna at Nelson@dot.com

Let's Talk!

Join the
Club

We meet the first Sunday of every month.
Bring your own rope, equipment, shoes, lunch.
Transportation provided.
Call 756-4177 for details.

WELCOME TO THE
CLUB

EVERY SATURDAY NIGHT
A DIFFERENT STYLE EVERY WEEK
FREE LESSONS
BRING YOUR FAVORITE CDs
CALL BRIDGET AT 520-1928

CLUB
You Oughta Be In Pictures!

• First and third Wednesdays
• Darkroom provided
• $15/month for supplies
• You pay for film
• Gallery space available

Call Tom at 656-3843

What are the four clubs above? Fill in the blanks in the ads with the following words.

(**Camera**) (**English**) (**Climbing**) (**Dance**)

Which words in each ad helped you decide? List them.

Camera Club _____   Climbing Club _____

English Club _____   Dance Club _____

---

*T*alk About It

◯ Have you ever belonged to a club? What was it? What did you do?

◯ Do you like belonging to clubs? Why or why not?

◯ Do you have an interest that would be a good idea for a club? What is it?

1 Vocabulary Review

A Fill in the chart with the names of the sports and hobbies you learned in this unit. Can you add any more?

Sports	Hobbies

B How many of these activities do you do? Are there any you would like to try?

I'd like to join the drama club.

Can I have your name, please?

2 Grammar Review

A Fill in the blanks.

1. _____ _____ help you?
2. Can _____ have your name, _____?
3. Can you give _____ _____ address, please?
4. How _____ _____ spell that, please?
5. Can _____ tell _____ your phone number, please?

B Unscramble the sentences and write them correctly.

1. please/I/have/can/address/your   _____
2. I/you/can/help   _____
3. your/fax/what's/please/number   _____
4. me/your/tell/name/you/please/can   _____
5. can/your/you/me/number/give/telephone/please   _____

3 Log On

Practice more with the language and topics you studied on the *Expressions* website:

http://expressions.heinle.com

I have two older sisters.

1 Get Ready

A Look at the information about Sylvia and Jerry. Which picture shows Sylvia's family? Which shows Jerry's? Write the correct number in the circles below.

Jerry's Family

Jerry

mother

father

two sisters

grandmother

Sylvia's Family

Sylvia

mother

father

B What other family words can you name using the pictures above? Make a list with a partner. Can you think of any others?

Family words

2 Start Talking

A Look at the conversation and listen.

Sylvia: How many people are there in your family?

Jerry: There are six of us—me, my mother and father, my two sisters, and my grandmother. How about you?

Sylvia: Just three—me, my mom and my dad.

Pair work

B Practice with a partner.
Then practice again using the other family pictures in Get Ready.

3 Listen In

(A) Do you have any brothers or sisters? Are they older or younger? Tell your partner.

(B) Listen. How many times do you hear these words? Check (✔) each time you hear them.

1. brother _____   **3.** sister _____
2. brothers _____   **4.** sisters _____

(C) Listen again. Which is Alicia's family? Which is Patrick's family?
Write the person's name under the correct picture.

Try this ....
**Look at the pictures.
Which person do you
think is Alicia? Which
do you think is Patrick?**

4 Say It Right

(A) Listen and underline the word with the heaviest stress in each reply.

1. A: Is Carol your older sister?
   B: No, she's my <u>younger</u> sister.

2. A: Is Jimmy the youngest child in the family?
   B: No, Jason is the youngest.

3. A: Do you have three brothers?
   B: No, I have four.

4. A: Is Susan your sister?
   B: No, she's my cousin.

5. A: Does Helen have an older sister?
   B: No, she has an older brother.

(B) Listen again and practice.

Try this ....
**Write two conversations like
the ones above. Read your
sentences to your partner.
Your partner will tell you which
word is stressed.**

I have two older sisters.

5 Focus In

(A) Look at the chart.

Questions with _How many_	
How many people **are there** in your family?	**There are** five.
How many brothers and sisters **do you have**?	**I have** three.
	I have two older sisters and a younger brother.
	I don't have any. I'm an only child.

(B) Number the sentences to make a conversation.

_____1_____ How many people are there in your family?

_____ Only three—me, my mom and my dad.

_____ Two of my sisters. How many people are there in your family?

_____ How many of them are older than you?

_____ There are seven of us. I have three sisters and a brother.

(C) Add three questions to make a family survey. Then ask a partner the questions.

1. How many people are there in your family?
2. How many brothers do you have?
3. _____?
4. _____?
5. _____?

6 Talk Some More

Spotlight
You can also say _elder sister_ instead of _older sister_.

(A) Write the words in the correct spaces.

Alison: How _____ brothers and sisters do you have?

Paul: I have two _____ sisters.

Alison: Do _____ all live together?

Paul: No, my _____ sister is married.

_____ lives with her _____ in Florida.

she   you   oldest

many   family   older

(B) Check your answers.

Pair work **(C) Practice the conversation with a partner.
Then practice again, using your own information.**

Work In Pairs — Student A

A) Look at the photo of Kevin's family. How many brothers and sisters does Kevin have? Which are older, do you think? Which are younger?

Kevin

B) Your partner has a photo of Annette's family. Ask your partner questions and find the differences between the two families. List the differences below.

Kevin
_____
_____
_____

Annette
_____
_____
_____

C) How many differences did you find? Check your list with your partner.

Try this

Make up a family of your own.
List the family members below. Try the exercise again.

_____
_____

I have two older sisters.

7 Work In Pairs ⟨Student B⟩

A Look at the photo of Annette's family. How many brothers and sisters does Annette have? Which are older, do you think? Which are younger?

Annette

B Your partner has a photo of Kevin's family. Ask your partner questions and find the differences between the two families. List the differences below.

Annette	Kevin
_____	_____
_____	_____
_____	_____

C How many differences did you find? Check your list with your partner.

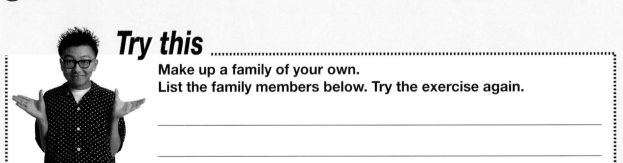

Try this

Make up a family of your own.
List the family members below. Try the exercise again.

_____

_____

8 Express Yourself

A Survey. Ask your classmates questions to find the information.
Write a different person's name in each space.

Find someone who...

	Name		Name
has an older sister		is an only child	
is the youngest child		has an older brother	
has no sisters		has a younger brother	
has a younger sister		has no brothers	

Group work **B** Share your information with a partner.

This is Aunt Mary.

9 Think About It

In many cultures, people have special ways of calling members of their family. In English-speaking cultures, most people call their grandparents by their title only, such as **Grandfather** and **Grandmother**. Aunts and uncles are usually called by their name and title, such as **Aunt Kathy** or **Uncle John**. Brothers and sisters are called by their name, not by a title.

• *How about in your culture? How do you call the different members of your family?*

10 Write About It

A Look at the note.

Dear Mr. and Mrs. Smith,

Thank you for agreeing to be my host family. I'm looking forward to going to the United States very much.
Here is a photo of my family. As you can see, I have two sisters and two brothers...

B Imagine that you are going to stay with a host family in the United States.
Write a note on a separate piece of paper using your own information.

I have two older sisters. **21**

11 Read On — Family Reunions

• *Strategy: Scanning*

Family reunions are popular in many parts of the world.
What kinds of things do families do at reunions?

Anita Summerlin, Linden, Texas, U.S.A.
When I was a child, we had family reunions in September. About 100 people came to our farmhouse. Everyone brought food and we cooked together. We ate at long tables outside. The children took care of the ice cream maker. We took walks and told stories and took photographs and sang songs. Everyone had such a good time.

Elena Lopez, Cartagena, Colombia
Our family has a reunion every two years. We always rent three houses at the beach. There are 23 of us. Everyone brings food, and we prepare it together. In the daytime some of us swim, some take long walks, some just talk to each other. In the evenings we have performances. Everyone has to do something: dance, or sing a song, or tell a good story. We always make a video to remember our reunions.

Khaled Al-Youssef, Kuwait City, Kuwait
We have a really BIG family reunion every five years. More than 200 people came to the last one. Some of them flew in from foreign countries. We meet at my uncle's house, which is very large. Everyone brings food, and we eat together. The kids play and the adults talk. We show each other our pictures and we always take more. It's great to be a part of such a big family.

Check (✔) the correct column. In which family reunion(s) do the people...

	Summerlin	Lopez	Al-Youssef
come from foreign countries?			
bring food?			
take pictures?			
go swimming?			
take walks?			
tell stories?			
sing songs?			
make a video?			

Talk About It

🔘 How many people are there in your immediate family (your parents and brothers and sisters)?

🔘 Does your family ever get together for reunions? Where? What do you do?

🔘 Who is your favorite relative (outside your immediate family)? Why?

12 Review

1 Vocabulary Review

A Fill in the chart with the family words you learned in this unit.

Male	Female

B How many of these people are there in your family?

How many brothers and sisters do you have?

Oh... just one.

2 Grammar Review

A Draw lines to match the questions and answers.

1. Do you all live together?
2. Is Ali your older brother?
3. Do you have two brothers?
4. Is Maria your daughter?
5. Does Pedro have a younger brother?

a. No, he has a younger sister.
b. No, she's my sister.
c. Yes, we do.
d. No, I have only one.
e. No, he's my younger brother.

B Fill in the blanks and answer the questions. Use your own information.

1. How many people _____ _____ in your family?
_____

2. How many brothers and sisters _____ you _____ ?
_____

3. How _____ are older. How _____ are younger?
_____

4. _____ _____ all live together?
_____

3 Log On

Practice more with the language and topics you studied on the *Expressions* website:

http://expressions.heinle.com

What are you doing over the break?

1 Get Ready

A Write the number of the activity next to the correct picture (1–6).

1. take a cooking class
2. take driving lessons
3. study English
4. take singing lessons
5. take a swimming class
6. study computers

B What other classes do people take in your country? Make a list with a partner.

Types of classes

_____

_____

2 Start Talking 📼

A Look at the conversation and listen.

Glenda: What are you doing over the break?
Valerie: I'm going to take a swimming class.
Glenda: Oh, really? Where?
Valerie: At the Plaza Fitness Center.
Glenda: That sounds like fun.

Pair work

B Practice the conversation with a partner.
Then practice again, using different activities from Get Ready.

3 Listen In

A Which of the items in this list are indoor activities? Which are outdoor activities? Which are neither?

driving	visit	surfing
watch videos	Denver	home
sports center	watch TV	computer
computer school	mountains	golf
tennis	health club	skiing

B Listen and circle the words you hear.

C Listen again and fill in the chart.

	What?	Where?
Rick		
Amy		
Suzanne		
Phil		

4 Say It Right

A In rapid speech, *going to* is sometimes reduced to sound like *gonna*. Listen and check (✔) the sentences where *going to* is reduced.

1. _____ Are you going to visit your family over the break?
2. _____ I'm going to meet some friends after work.
3. _____ Where are you going to buy her birthday gift?
4. _____ They're going to pick us up on their way to work.
5. _____ My boss is going to stop by at 7:00.

Try this

Make up three more sentences using *going to*. Then practice the reduced pronunciation with a partner.

B Listen again and practice.

What are you doing over the break?   **25**

5 Focus In

A **Look at the chart.**

Present continuous for future	
What are you doing over the break?	**I'm taking** a computer class. **I'm taking** piano lessons.
Are you doing anything this weekend?	Yes, **I'm visiting** the relatives. No, **I'm staying** at home.

B **Complete the conversations using *doing* or *going*.**

A: Are you _____ anything over the break?

B: Yes, I'm _____ on vacation with my family to Japan.

A: Oh, really? What are you _____ in Japan?

B: Well, first we're _____ to Tokyo for a few days.
Then, we're _____ down to Osaka on the bullet train.

A: Sounds great. Are you _____ any sightseeing in Kyoto?

B: Yeah, we're _____ there, too, if we have time.

C **Make questions using the words shown. Then ask a partner.**

1. Where/going/break? _____
2. When/going? _____
3. What/doing/there? _____
4. Who/going/with? _____

6 Talk Some More

A **Number the sentences to make a conversation (1–5).**

Lisa: _____ About a week. How about you?

Henry: _____ Are you going anywhere over the break?

Henry: _____ Oh, I don't really have any plans.

Lisa: _____ Yes, we're going to the beach.

Henry: _____ How long are you staying there?

B **Check your answers.**

C **Practice the conversation with a partner.**
Then practice again using your own information.

Work In Pairs 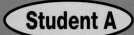 Student A

Student B: Use page 28

A Look at the activities in the pictures below. What are they?
How long does each one last?

Painting Class
ARRABI
SCHOOL OF
FINE ARTS
July 1-31

Brenda

Intensive Course
French
French Cultural Center
July 1-15

Laura

Golf Lessons
for Beginners
Westmont Country Club
July 8-10

Donald

HIKING TOUR
Mt. Winnebago
July 16-17

Calvin

B Ask your partner questions and fill in the information about these people's plans.

	Activity	Where/How long
Joseph		
Louise		
Wilma		
Scott		

C Answer your partner's questions about the activities in the pictures above.

Is Mary doing anything over the break?

Yes! She's going out with me.

Try this ...

Make up new plans for Brenda, Laura, Donald and Calvin. Try the exercise again.

_____

_____

What are you doing over the break?

Work In Pairs Student B

A Look at the activities in the pictures below. What are they?
How long does each one last?

Scott   Wilma   Louise   Joseph

B Answer your partner's questions about
the activities in the pictures above.

Is Mary doing anything over the break?

Yes! She's going out with me.

C Ask your partner questions
and fill in the information about
these people's plans.

	Activity	Where/How long
Calvin		
Donald		
Laura		
Brenda		

Try this

Make up new plans for Scott, Wilma, Louise and Joseph. Try the exercise again.

8 Express Yourself

(A) What are your plans? Write your answers in the column marked *You*.

What are you doing...	You	Student 1	Student 2
after class?			
tonight?			
on Saturday?			
on Sunday?			

(B) Ask two classmates the questions and note their answers in the columns.

Group work **(C)** Share your information. How many people have the same plans as you?

I'm going out for coffee after class.

9 Think About It

    In the U.S. and Canada, students usually enjoy two or three months' summer vacation. They usually have a week or two in winter and one week in spring. Many students do part-time jobs, go on trips or even study. Break time plans are a popular conversation topic among students of all ages.

- *How much vacation time do students get in your country? What do they normally do?*

10 Write About It

(A) Look at the note.

(B) On a separate piece of paper, write about your plans for your next vacation.

This summer I'm going to Greece with two of my friends from work. I always wanted to visit Athens, and this is my big chance. We are planning to visit all the famous historical sights, and we are also taking a trip to some of the islands.

Group work **(C)** Share your plans. Whose sound the most exciting?

• *Strategy: Inferring vocabulary*

If you have no special plans for your break, why not give your time away?

Don't listen to people who say that teenagers today are selfish. It's not true, say many charities. Volunteering is on the rise in the United States. Millions of teenagers spend their school holidays helping others. And they do it for free. Here are some of their stories:

Jason Moore, 18
This summer, I'm going to volunteer with Habitat for Humanity. They build good, low-cost houses and sell them to needy families at no profit. They've built over 90,000 houses in 60 countries. They'll teach me what to do, so I'll be helping people and also learning new skills.

Alice Hamilton, 18
I'm going to help the Forest Service build new hiking trails in the mountains of Idaho. It's going to be terrific —I'll spend the whole summer living in a tent and breathing the clean mountain air. I'm going to be sleeping under the stars, getting a great workout, *and* doing something good at the same time!

Trish Anderson, 16
I'm going to teach kids who have trouble reading. I'll be working for a program called Reading For Life. Every day, I'm going to be helping kids select and read books that interest them. I want to be a teacher, and I love children and reading, so this is going to be a great experience for me.

Find a word that means...

1. organizations that help needy causes (1 word) _____
2. giving your time for free (1 word) _____
3. money you make after paying expenses (1 word) _____
4. choose (1 word) _____
5. a path for walking (1 word) _____

Talk About It . . . .

○ Is volunteering common in your country? What kind of things do volunteers do?

○ Imagine you are going to volunteer for something. What would you enjoy doing?

○ Volunteering helps others. But how is it good for the volunteer? What do you think?

12 Review

1 Vocabulary Review

A Fill in the chart with the activities you learned in this unit.

Indoor activities	Outdoor activities

B Which of these activities have you done? Which ones would you like to do?

Are you doing anything over the break?

I'm taking piano lessons.

2 Grammar Review

A Answer the questions.

1. What are you doing after class today? _____
2. What are you doing tonight? _____
3. Are you doing anything tomorrow night? _____
4. Are you doing anything on Saturday? _____
5. What are you doing on Sunday? _____

B Unscramble the sentences to make a conversation.

1. anywhere/you/over/are/break/the/going

_____

2. beach/yes/to/going/the/we're _____
3. there/how/you/staying/long/are _____
4. week/a/about _____
5. sounds/wow/that/great _____

3 Log On

Practice more with the language and topics you studied on the *Expressions* website:

http://expressions.heinle.com

Goals
○ Asking and talking about vacation activities

Where did you go on vacation?

1 Get Ready

(A) Write the number of the activity next to the correct picture (1–8).

1. go hiking
2. stay in a nice hotel
3. see a concert
4. go sightseeing
5. go to a museum
6. go shopping
7. eat good food
8. go swimming

(B) Which of the activities can you do in each of these places?
Think of one more activity for each place. Share your ideas with a partner.

in the city   in the country   in the mountains   at the beach

2 Start Talking

(A) Look at the conversation and listen.

Martin: Where did you go on vacation?
Kelly: We went to the beach.
Martin: Did you have a good time?
Kelly: Yes, it was great.

Pair work

(B) Practice the conversation with a partner.
Then practice again using different places and activities from Get Ready.

3 Listen In

A Unscramble these four U.S. place names and write them in the correct spaces.

laslaD
ridloaF
Miima
sTeax

Cities

_____

_____

States

_____

_____

B Listen and number the questions in the order you hear them (1–4).

_____ Did you have a good time?

_____ Did you go anywhere?

_____ Where did you go?

_____ What did you do?

I went to Miami.

Where did you
go on vacation?

C Listen again and fill in the chart.

	Where?	What?	Good time?		
Bonnie			☺	☹	😐
Pete			☺	☹	😐

4 Say It Right

A Is the intonation rising (↗) or falling(↘)?
Listen and draw arrows to indicate rising or falling intonation at the end of the questions.

1. Where did you go on vacation? _____
2. Did you have a good time there? _____
3. What did you do in Mexico? _____
4. How was your vacation? _____
5. Did you go anywhere during the holiday? _____

B Listen again and practice.

Try this

What difference does a rising or falling intonation make to the meaning? Discuss it with the class.

Where did you go on vacation?

5 Focus In

A Look at the chart.

Questions and statements using simple past

Where did you go on vacation?	**I went** to Chicago.
What did you do in Chicago?	**I saw** a basketball game.
When did you get back?	**I got back** yesterday.
Did you go anywhere last weekend?	Yes, **I went t**o the beach.
Who did you go with?	**I went** with my family.
Did you have a good time?	Yeah, **it was** great.

B Circle the mistakes in these conversations and write the correct form in the spaces provided. If the sentence is correct, check (✔).

A: When did you got back? _____
B: Last night. _____
A: Did you went with Bill? _____
B: No, I go with my cousin. _____

A: Who you go to Mexico with? _____
B: A couple of friends. _____
A: Did you enjoyed the trip? _____
B: Yes, I enjoyed it a lot. _____

C Make up questions for these answers. Then ask a partner the questions.

1. _____? Yes, I did.
2. _____? We went to Spain.
3. _____? With my family.
4. _____? It was OK.

6 Talk Some More

Spotlight

That sounds nice. and Wow! That's great. are two ways to express interest.

A Write the words in the correct spaces.

Martin: What _____ you do at the beach?
Kelly: We _____ swimming and hiking.
Martin: That sounds nice.
Kelly: Yes, it _____. Did you _____ anywhere?
Martin: We went to Chicago. We went to some museums, _____ good food, and _____ a basketball game.
Kelly: Wow! That's great.

saw   was   went   did   ate   go

B Check your answers.

Pair work

C Practice the conversation with a partner. Then practice again using other vacation activities.

Work In Pairs   Student A

Student B: Use page 36

A Imagine these are items from your last vacation. Which item is related to shopping? To musicals? And to eating out? Label them correctly.

Broadway Spectacular
ADMIT ONE
Miss Saigon
FRIDAY, 14 JUNE
66010

NEW YORK CITY
Guide to Shopping
Your Guide to All the Best the City has to Offer

New York City
Restaurant Guide
Randy's Steak House
5th Avenue NY
Bayview Restaurant
Longwood NY

B Ask questions about your partner's vacation and fill in the chart.

Where?	What?	Good time?

C Now answer your partner's questions about your last vacation.

Where did Joy go on vacation?

She went to Paris.

Try this

Imagine you and your partner recently visited a big city. Decide where you went and think of three things you did there. Make a list. Tell another pair about your vacation.

1 _____

2 _____

3 _____

Work In Pairs Student B

A Imagine these are items from your last vacation. Which item is related to sightseeing? To a famous house? And to an art museum? Label them correctly.

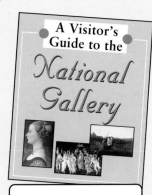

B Answer your partner's questions about your last vacation.

C Now ask questions about your partner's vacation and fill in the chart.

Where?	What?	Good time?

Try this

Imagine you and your partner recently visited a big city. Decide where you went and think of three things you did there. Make a list. Tell another pair about your vacation.

1 _____
2 _____
3 _____

8 Express Yourself

A Survey three classmates. Ask questions about their last vacation and fill in the chart.

Student 1	Student 2	Student 3

 B Share your information with your classmates. Decide who had the most interesting vacation.

I brought you something from Australia.

9 Think About It

Souvenirs from vacations are more important in some cultures than in others.

• *When you go on vacation, who do you usually buy souvenirs for?*

— *Family members*   — *Friends*
— *Co-workers/Classmates*   — *Boss/Teacher*
— *Neighbors*   — *A pet*

• *What kind of souvenirs do you buy?*

10 Write About It

A Look at the postcard.

> Hi everybody,
>
> I never knew that Miami could be so much fun. Yesterday we went deep sea fishing, and I caught a shark. Last night we went to see the Miami Dolphins— they lost!
>
> The weather here is perfect. Hope the rain has stopped at home.
>
> Say hello to the boss for me.
>
> See you soon,
> Lillian
>
> AYE Rentals
> 157 Byrd Street
> Chiswick, CH4 3UJ
> England

B You are having the best vacation of your life. Send a postcard to your classmates.

Read On   Active Vacations

• *Strategy: Scanning*

If you're the active type, maybe you don't want to spend your vacation lying by the pool or visiting museums. Maybe you should try what these people did...

Kim Suk-ki, *architect* —————————————————————————————————

Last summer, I went rafting with River Adventures. The guides teach you how to handle a raft safely, and then they take you down some really beautiful rivers. It's safe but exciting! At night, the guides cook your dinner while you relax, hike, or play on the shore. The food is great, and you'll never forget the views.

Mercedes Cruz, *store manager* ————————————————————————————

For my last summer vacation, I went to Copenhagen on a cycling holiday. After arriving, I met a representative from Cycling Vacations. She provided me with a bike, a road map, a ferryboat schedule, and a list of inns and restaurants. Then I took a ferry to the nearby islands. It's great—you set the schedule, you decide where to go, and where to stay and eat. At the end of my vacation, I was more relaxed than I'd ever been before. You should try it!

Mary O'Brien, *writer* ——————————————————————————————————

I spent my vacation at Dolphin Bay. It's a coral reef where you can play among lots of colorful fish. Best of all, you can swim among real dolphins. It's such a thrill! And it's only a few steps from the water to your room. Our hotel was the best in south Florida—the kitchen staff there has won prizes for their food.

Are the following statements True or False? Check (✔).	True	False
1. At Dolphin Bay, you can swim with colorful fish.	☐	☐
2. River Adventures offers you a swimming vacation.	☐	☐
3. You'll need to bring your own bike for a Cycling Vacation.	☐	☐
4. The hotel at Dolphin Bay is close to the coral reef.	☐	☐
5. You have to cook your own food for all of these vacations.	☐	☐
6. A River Adventures vacation is active, but not dangerous.	☐	☐

*T*alk About It ....

○ What's the best vacation you've ever taken? Where did you go? Why was it so good?

○ Which of these vacations do you think you'd like best? Why?

○ What's a place in the world that you dream of traveling to? What would you like to do there?

12 Review

1 Vocabulary Review

A Fill in the chart with the vacation activities you learned in this unit.

In the city	In the mountains	At the beach

B Which of these things do you like to do on vacation?

What did you do in New York?

Everything!

2 Grammar Review

A Complete the questions and match with the best response.

1. _____ you go anywhere last summer?
2. _____ did you do there?
3. _____ did you go with?
4. _____ did you get back?
5. _____ have a good time?

a. My girlfriend.
b. Yes, I went to Thailand.
c. Yeah, it was great.
d. Just last night.
e. We went elephant trekking.

B Answer the questions. Write complete sentences.

1. Where did you go on your last vacation? _____

2. What did you do there? Write about three activities.

_____

_____

_____

3 Log On

Practice more with the language and topics you studied on the *Expressions* website:

http://expressions.heinle.com

Can I help you?

1 Get Ready

A Write the number of the item next to the correct item in the picture (1–8).

1.	newspaper	$1.75
2.	roll of film	$4.29
3.	pack of tissues	$.80
4.	candy bar	$.65
5.	magazine	$3.95
6.	postcard	$.50
7.	map	$5.99
8.	pack of gum	$.50

B *One newspaper. Two newspapers.* **What are the plural forms for the other words on the list?**

2 Start Talking

A Look at the conversation and listen.

Jackie: Can I help you?
Pete: Can I have a pack of gum and one of those newspapers, please?
Jackie: Sure. Here you go.
Pete: How much is that?
Jackie: That comes to $2.25 all together.
Pete: OK. Here you are.
Jackie: Thank you.

Pair work **B** Practice the conversation with a partner. Then practice again using different items from Get Ready.

3 Listen In

A What are the names of these items? Don't look back to Get Ready!

B Listen and check (✔) the items each time they are mentioned.

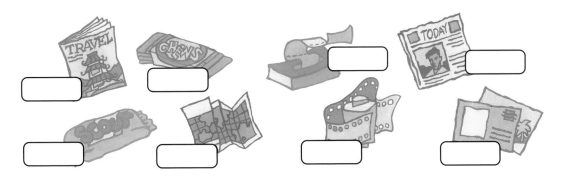

C Listen again and number the receipts (1–4).

Qty.	Item	Price
1	candy bar	$.75
1	map	$5.50
1	film	$5.10
	TOTAL	$11.35
	CASH	$12.00
	CHANGE	$.65

Jane Mart
Mc Donald St., West Triangle

Qty.	Item	Price
1	magazine	$3.95
1	gum	$.40
	TOTAL	$4.35
	CASH	$4.35
	CHANGE	$.00

GOOD MART

Qty.	Item	Price
1	magazine	$3.95
1	gum	$.59
1	newspaper	$.75
	TOTAL	$5.29
	CASH	$10.00
	CHANGE	$4.71

Donna's
Convenience Store
40595 Benjamin St. Augustin

QTY.	ITEM	PRICE
1	film	$4.95
1	newspaper	$1.00
1	tissue	$.85
	TOTAL	$6.80
	CASH	$7.00
	CHANGE	$.20

KEN-D STORE
5 HOPE STREET NEWTON

4 Say It Right

A In rapid speech, some numbers can be reduced.
Check (✔) the price that has reduced sounds in each pair.

1. _____ $2.25   _____ $2.25
2. _____ $4.79   _____ $4.79
3. _____ $23.99   _____ $23.99
4. _____ $3.80   _____ $3.80
5. _____ $46.29   _____ $46.29

Try this

Write five prices. Practice saying your prices to a partner. Use reduced sounds. Your partner will write the prices.

B Listen again and practice.

5 Focus In

A Look at the chart.

> Can I have another can of tuna, please?

Quantifiers

Can I have **a pack of** cookies?

May I have **a bottle of** ketchup?

A kilo of potatoes, please.

I'll take **a can of** tuna.

I'll have **a jar of** salsa, please.

B How do we ask for these things? Write each item next to the correct container (in some cases, there may be more than one correct answer).

1. A jar of _____
2. A can of _____
3. A pack of _____
4. A bottle of _____
5. A kilo of _____

chicken   cheese   jam

salad oil   spaghetti   olives

beans   water   onions

C Circle the mistakes. Then write correct sentences.

1. Could I have a bottle of beans, please?   _____
2. Can I have a kilo of film, please?   _____
3. A pack of mayonnaise, please.   _____
4. Can I have a can of chewing gum, please?   _____

6 Talk Some More

A Number the sentences to make a conversation (1–7).

Keith: ___1___ Anything else for you today?

Sandra: _____ Cash.

Keith: _____ That comes to $17.58.

Keith: _____ Cash or credit card?

Sandra: _____ No, thanks. That'll be all.

Sandra: _____ Here you go.

Keith: _____ Out of $20, your change is $2.42. Here you are. Thank you very much.

B Check your answers.

C Practice the conversation with a partner. Then practice again using different prices.

Work In Pairs · Student A

Student B: Use page 44

A Write three prices.
Add them up.
Write the total.

1. _____
2. _____
3. _____
Total _____

B Say your prices to your partner. Don't give the total. Your partner will tell you!

C Ask your partner for the prices at Quick Shop and write them.
Then answer your partner's questions.

Things to buy...	Cost Right	Quick Shop
1 pack of spaghetti	$1.00	_____
1 can of tomato sauce	$.75	_____
1 loaf of bread	$.99	_____
1 head of lettuce	$.99	_____
1 pack of cheese	$1.75	_____
1 bottle of salad dressing	$1.50	_____
1 kilo of ground beef	$2.99	_____
1 bottle of water	$1.00	_____

Can I help you?

Yes. How much is the store?

Try this

You and your partner are going shopping. Together, you have $10 to spend. Decide where you will buy each item on the list.

_____

_____

_____

A Write three prices.
Add them up.
Write the total.

1. _____
2. _____
3. _____
Total _____

B Say your prices to your partner. Don't give the total. Your partner will tell you!

C Answer your partner's questions.
Then ask your partner for the prices at Cost Right and write them.

Things to buy...	Quick Shop	Cost Right
1 pack of spaghetti	$2.00	_____
1 can of tomato sauce	$1.50	_____
1 loaf of bread	$ .75	_____
1 head of lettuce	$ .75	_____
1 pack of cheese	$3.99	_____
1 bottle of salad dressing	$1.75	_____
1 kilo of ground beef	$1.99	_____
1 bottle of water	$.75	_____

Can I help you?

Yes. How much is the store?

Try this

You and your partner are going shopping. Together, you have $10 to spend. Decide where you will buy each item on the list.

_____

_____

_____

8 Express Yourself

A What do you think is the correct price for each item? Write the price next to each one.

$.50 $.99 $1.00 $1.99 $3.00 $3.75

Group work

B Imagine you want to buy each item above.
Find out who in your group has the best price for each.

C Practice buying the items. On a piece of paper, write down the prices.
How much did you spend in total?

9 *Think About It*

Around the world, more and more people are becoming concerned about the environment. Many customers now carry their own shopping bags, so the store doesn't have to use disposable ones. Sometimes clerks ask, ***Do you need a bag?***

• *How about in your culture? Are shoppers becoming more environmentally friendly?*

10 Write About It

A Look at the recipe for hamburgers.

Recipe

What you need:
• 500 grams of ground beef
• 1 onion—finely chopped
• salt and pepper to taste
• lettuce—shredded
• ketchup and mustard
• buns
• cooking oil

What you do:
Mix together the ground beef, onion, salt and pepper. Form it into patties. Put a little oil in a large frying pan, and heat it. When it reaches medium heat, put in the patties and fry until done. Serve on buns with lettuce, ketchup and mustard.

B On a piece of paper, write out the recipe for your favorite dish.

Read On A World Famous Market

• *Strategy: Analyzing word parts*

What's the most interesting market you've ever visited? Shoppers in Barcelona have only one answer.

Photo by Miguel Raurich
© Turisme de Barcelona

Dear Sheryl,

Greetings from Barcelona! I'm having a great time here.
Today I found the most unbelievable market near my hotel. It's called 'La Boqueria.'

From the outside it looks like a railway station. But inside, there are countless market stalls. There were piles of colorful fruits and vegetables everywhere. Some of them were completely unknown to me. There were also breads, cheeses, meats, dried fruits and nuts. In the middle was the seafood section. Amazing!

I stood there speechless. I can't find the words to describe the sights and sounds and smells. I wanted to buy everything! But I could never eat so much food! So I sat down at a little snack bar and ordered three simple items.

One was a slice of toasted bread with tomato and garlic. The second was a slice of cheese made from sheep's milk. The last was a little dish of small brown olives. It wasn't much, but it was mouthwatering. In fact, I think it was the best lunch I've ever eaten.

Sometimes a word can be broken into smaller words. When we look at the smaller words, we can understand the longer word. Check (✔) the best meaning.

Example: seafood = sea + food   Food from the ocean

1. unbelievable (Paragraph 1) = un + believe + able   _____ *easy to believe*
_____ *hard to believe*

2. colorful (Paragraph 2) = color + full   _____ *all the same color*
_____ *lots of colors*

3. speechless (Paragraph 3) = speech + less   _____ *without talking*
_____ *talking a lot*

4. mouthwatering (Paragraph 4) = mouth + watering   _____ *very wet*
_____ *very delicious*

Talk About It

🔵 Where's your favorite market? What do you like about it?

🔵 What kinds of large markets have you visited?

🔵 What's the most interesting thing you've ever seen at a market?

Review

1 Vocabulary Review

A Fill in the chart with the shopping items you learned in this unit.

Food	Drink	Others

I need a loaf of bread now!

B How often do you go food shopping? What do you usually buy?

2 Grammar Review

A How do we usually ask for these items? Fill in the blanks.

1. ___a___ ___pack___ ___of___ gum
2. _____ _____ _____ film
3. _____ _____ _____ tomato sauce
4. _____ _____ _____ bread
5. _____ _____ _____ water
6. _____ _____ _____ lettuce

B You want a magazine ($3.50), a newspaper ($ .75) and a candy bar ($ .75). You pay with a $10 bill. Write the conversation you have with the salesclerk.

Salesclerk: Can I help you?

You: _____

Salesclerk: _____

You: How much is that?

Salesclerk: _____

You: Here you are.

Salesclerk: _____

You: Thank you.

3 Log On

Practice more with the language and topics you studied on the *Expressions* website:

http://expressions.heinle.com

Goals ·

○ *Describing occupations* ○ *Talking about likes and dislikes*

What do you do?

1 Get Ready

wendi shin
graphic designer
cd tech incorporated
darby, PA

HI-TEL TECHNOLOGIES

Cynthia Morales
Sales Manager

Camden, New Jersey

Edgewater Computer Institute

Thomas Miller
Teacher

Burlington, New Jersey

A Write the number of the workplace next to the correct business card.

1.	school
2.	office
3.	factory
4.	studio

Republic Industries
Chester, PA

Douglas Burton
Engineer

B Think of three people you know. Write their information in the spaces.

Name	Job	Workplace

2 Start Talking 🎞

A Look at the conversation and listen.

Cynthia: What do you do?
Douglas: I'm an engineer.
Cynthia: Oh, where do you work?
Douglas: I work for Republic Industries.
Cynthia: Oh, really? Where's that?
Douglas: Our factory is in Chester. Where do you work?
Cynthia: I work for Hi-Tel Technologies. I sell computers.

Pair work **B** Practice the conversation with a partner. Then practice again using the occupations on the business cards and the list you made.

3 Listen In

(A) Look at the jobs in the chart. In your country, are these jobs usually for men or women?
How about doctors? Nurses? Pilots? Salesclerks?

(B) Listen and match the name with the job and workplace. Draw lines.

Name	Job	Workplace
1. Gloria	designer	Idea One, Inc.
2. Daniel	receptionist	Head Start Academy
3. Richard	salesperson	Waterford & Simmons
4. Susan	teacher	DSA Properties

(C) Listen again.
Do these people like their job?
Check (✔) *yes, no* or
yes and no.

	Yes	No	Yes & no
1. Gloria			
2. Daniel			
3. Richard			
4. Susan			

4 Say It Right

(A) Intonation can be used to change the meaning of a sentence.
Listen to the examples.

Example 1:
A: Do you like your job?
B: It's OK.

Example 2:
A: Do you like your job?
B: It's OK.

	Likes	Dislikes
Example 1	✔	
Example 2		✔
1.		
2.		
3.		
4.		

(B) Listen to the responses and
check (✔) *likes* or *dislikes.*

(C) Listen again and practice
the responses.

5 Focus In

A **Look at the chart.**

Like + ___ing and get to + verb

What's your job like?	It's great. I **like working** in an office.
Do you like your job?	It's OK, but I don't **like traveling** very much.
	It's wonderful. I **get to meet** a lot of interesting people.
	Not really. I **don't get to travel** very much.

B **Check (✔) the correct sentence in each pair.**

1. _____ Does he get to study English for free at his company?

   _____ Does he gets to study English for free at his company?

2. _____ He doesn't really liking to work outdoors.

   _____ He doesn't really like working outdoors.

3. _____ Does she like working the morning shift?

   _____ Is she like working the morning shift?

4. _____ They get to going on a company trip every summer.

   _____ They get to go on a company trip every summer.

C **Unscramble the questions. Then ask your partner.**

1. English/a lot/get to/do/you/practice _____

2. you/like/studying/on/do/the weekends _____

3. you/get/in/English/watch/videos/do/to _____

4. like/you/taking/do/tests _____

6 Talk Some More

(travel) (working) (meet)

(job) (traveling) (interesting)

A **Write the words in the correct spaces.**

Gerald: What's your _____ like?

Cynthia: It's pretty _____.

   I get to _____ and _____

   a lot of people. Do you like your job?

Gerald: Yes, it's all right.

   I like _____ in an office.

   I don't like _____ very much.

B **Check your answers.**

Spotlight

I get to... is positive. It is used to talk about a nice part of your job.

C **Practice the conversation with a partner.**
Then practice again using one of the jobs in your list from Get Ready.

Work In Pairs — Student A

A Write your name in the business card.
Would you like to have this job? Think of some good or bad points about the job and write them.

Reliable Auto Parts, Inc.

Long Beach, California

_____

Sales Manager

I _____ my job because
_____
_____
_____

B Answer your partner's questions about your job.

C Ask about your partner's job and fill in the missing information.

Name: _____
Occupation: _____
Location: _____
Likes job? Why or why not? _____

Do you like your job?

Well, not really.

Try this

Would you like to have your partner's job? Why or why not?
Write your reasons.

_____
_____
_____

A Write your name in the business card.
Would you like to have this job? Think of some good or bad points about the job and write them.

KSDM RADIO

Santa Monica, California

Marketing Assistant

I _____ my job because
_____
_____

B Answer your partner's questions about your job.

C Ask about your partner's job and fill in the missing information.

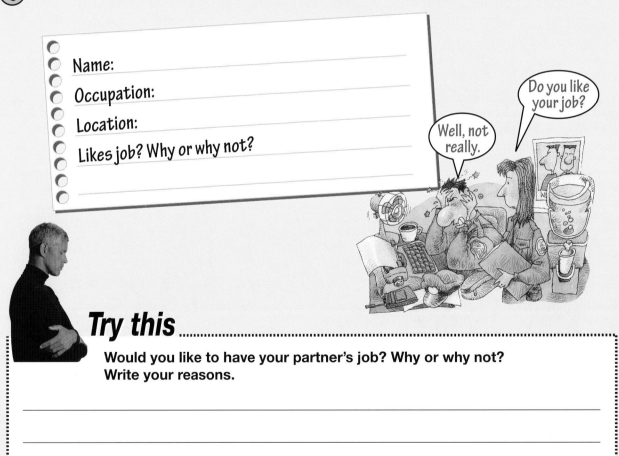

Name:

Occupation:

Location:

Likes job? Why or why not?

Well, not really.

Do you like your job?

Try this

Would you like to have your partner's job? Why or why not?
Write your reasons.

8 Express Yourself

(A) Write your own occupation or an occupation you'd like to have.
List some of the good and bad points about the job.

Job: _____	**Good points**	**Bad points**
	_____	_____
	_____	_____
	_____	_____

Group work

(B) Ask your partners about their jobs. What do they like or dislike?

(C) Work with someone from another group.
Answer the questions.

1. *What jobs did your group talk about?*
2. *Which of these jobs would you like/dislike? Why?*

Here's my card.

9 Think About It

Exchanging business cards is a common custom in many cultures.
In some cultures, there are many formal rules about doing this. In other cultures, it's more casual. But when you meet someone from another culture for the first time, it's important to know the rules.

• *How about in your culture? Are there special rules for exchanging business cards?*

10 Write About It

(A) Look at the information in the job application.

> I would like to work for the San Diego Zoo because I enjoy working outdoors, and I love animals.
> I have several pets at home.
> When I was growing up, I always wanted to work at a zoo or for a veterinarian.

(B) On a piece of paper, write a similar paragraph about your ideal job.
Then share it with your classmates.

• *Strategy: Reviewing*

What's an invention that's really useful to people everywhere?

How would you use a radio or a telephone if you had no electricity or batteries? These problems bothered British inventor Trevor Baylis. So in 1996 he invented a wind-up radio. It doesn't need electricity or batteries. You wind it up by hand. It plays for about an hour. Then, you wind it up again. Today it's manufactured in South Africa.

Then in 1999, Baylis invented a mobile telephone that is powered by shoes. The shoes contain a small battery that is powered when you walk. This battery is connected to a mobile phone. These two simple inventions can bring modern communications to all parts of the world.

Baylis doesn't have a university degree in engineering. In fact, he left high school before graduating. He just loves making things to help people. He never knows when ideas will come to him. He got the idea for the radio while watching TV. The idea for the telephone came to him in a dream.

Make true sentences by combining one part from each column.

A	B	C
Trevor Baylis	is powered	by people around the world.
You wind up	come to him	at unexpected times.
The mobile phone	are used	high school.
These inventions	never finished	to make it play.
Baylis' ideas	the radio	by walking.

1. *Trevor Baylis never finished high school.* _____
2. _____
3. _____
4. _____
5. _____

---

*T*alk About It

⊙ An English proverb says: *Necessity is the mother of invention.* What do you think this means?

⊙ What is the most useful invention of the last 100 years? Why?

⊙ Do you have a good idea for an invention? What is it?

1 Vocabulary Review

(A) Fill in the chart with words you learned in this unit.

Jobs I like	Jobs I don't like

(B) Which jobs do members of your family do?
Do they like them?

Do you like your job?

It's OK, but I don't like getting up so early.

2 Grammar Review

(A) Rewrite the sentences using the words in parentheses.

1. I travel a lot. (don't get to) _I don't get to travel a lot._

2. I meet interesting people. (get to) _____

3. I work outdoors. (like) _____

4. I work in an office. (don't like) _____

5. I work on the weekends. (don't really like) _____

(B) Complete the sentences with nice things about each job.

1. I'm a sales manager. _I get to meet people and..._

2. I'm a pilot. _____

3. I'm a doctor. _____

4. I'm an artist. _____

5. I'm a musician. _____

3 Log On

Practice more with the language and topics you studied on the *Expressions* website:

http://expressions.heinle.com

Goals

○ *Making requests*   ○ *Thanking people*

Could you do me a favor?

1 Get Ready

A Write the number of the activity next to the correct picture (1–5).

1. type my presentation
2. make copies of my presentation
3. find the keys to the meeting room
4. carry some boxes to the meeting room
5. prepare the meeting room for my presentation

B Which of the following can you do by yourself? Which would you ask for help with? Compare your answers with a partner.

- *write my resume*
- *check my composition*
- *prepare for a test*
- *look for something on the Internet*

2 Start Talking

A Look at the conversation and listen.

Ally: Could you do me a favor?
Edwin: Sure. What is it?
Ally: Could you help me type my presentation?
Edwin: No problem.
Ally: Thanks a lot.

Pair work **B** Practice the conversation with a partner. Then practice again using the activities above.

3 Listen In

(A) Which of these are polite requests? Check (✔) them.

1. _____ Give me a hand.
2. _____ Could you do me a favor?
3. _____ Could you help me?

4. _____ Help me out for a minute.
5. _____ Could you lend me a hand?
6. _____ Help me, now!

(B) Listen and check (✔) the number of the conversation where you hear the following expressions.

	No. 1	No. 2	No. 3	No. 4
could you				
I need				
do you need				
thank you				
thanks				
don't mention it				

(C) Listen again and number the pictures (1–4).

4 Say It Right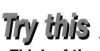

(A) *Could you* and *Do you* are often reduced in questions. Listen to the difference.

1. Could you do me a favor?
2. Could you help me for a minute?
3. Could you do something for me?
4. Do you need some help?
5. Do you need anything else?

Try this

Think of three more questions. Practice saying them to your partner. Your partner will say *reduced* or *not reduced*.

(B) Listen again and practice the questions in their reduced form.

5 Focus In

(A) Look at the chart.

Need and need to		
Do you **need**	some help?	Thanks. That would be great.
	to type your report?	Yes. Could you give me a hand?
I **need**	a copy of this document.	OK, sure. No problem.
	to see Mr. Clark.	Fine. I'll call him for you.

(B) Write the number of the statement next to the best response.

1. I need to find the meeting room.
2. We need to see the boss.
3. The boss needs her desk diary.
4. You need to call home at once.
5. I need some help.

_____ Sorry, I'm busy right now

_____ Do you have a cell phone?

_____ It's the second door on the left.

_____ I'm sorry, but she's in a meeting.

_____ It's on her desk.

(C) Finish the two conversations. Then practice them with a partner.

Conversation 1

A: Could you do me a favor?

B: Sure. What is it?

A: _____

B: _____

Conversation 2

A: Could you lend me a hand?

B: Sure. What do you need?

A: _____

B: _____

6 Talk Some More

(A) Number the sentences to make a conversation (1–5).

Jill: ___1___ Do you need some help?

Jill: _____ You're welcome.

Jill: _____ OK. I'll help you.

Nancy: _____ That would be great. I need to carry these boxes to the meeting room.

Nancy: _____ Great. Thank you.

Spotlight

Thanks and *Thanks a lot* are informal.
Thank you is neutral.
Thank you very much is formal.

(B) Check your answers.

Pair work

(C) Practice the conversation with a partner. Then practice again using other favors.

Work In Pairs Student A

Student B: Use page 60

A Look at the pictures. Write the missing verbs in the correct places. Which verb is left over?

(write) (do) (borrow) (study) (practice)

_____ for a test

_____ the piano

_____ a history report

_____ math homework

B Ask your partner for help with the activities in the pictures.

C Read the sentences. Then ask your partner for favors.

1. You forgot to bring money for lunch.
2. You forgot to bring your dictionary to class.
3. Your pencil just broke.
4. Your partner has a new video you want to see.

Could you guys do me a favor?

Sure. How can we help?

Try this

Is there anything you didn't want to or couldn't do for your partner?
What could you say in that situation?

_____

_____

7 Work In Pairs (Student B)

A Look at the pictures. Write the missing verbs in the correct places. Which verb is left over?

(feed)   (get)   (cook)   (clean)   (take out)

_____ dinner

_____ the garbage

_____ the dog

_____ the house

B Ask your partner for help with the activities in the pictures.

C Read the sentences. Then ask your partner for favors.

1. Your pen just ran out of ink.
2. You forgot to bring your notebook to class.
3. You're $1.00 short paying for lunch.
4. You didn't attend class yesterday and want the notes.

Could you guys do me a favor?

Sure. How can we help?

Try this

Is there anything you didn't want to or couldn't do for your partner? What could you say in that situation?

_____

_____

8 Express Yourself

A Decide one request to make to your classmates.
Write it here.

> My Request
> _____

Name	Request
1. _____	_____
2. _____	_____
3. _____	_____

B Offer to help three classmates.
Note the request
each person makes.

Group work

C What requests did your classmates make?
Share your information.

Would you mind
giving me a hand?

9 *Think About It*

When we make a request using **Can you...** or **Could you...**,
it means we are asking someone we know well. If we are asking someone we don't know
so well, we often use **Would you mind....**

• *Which would you use with the following people?*

_____ *A family member*   _____ *A friend*

_____ *A classmate/co-worker* _____ *Your teacher/boss*

_____ *A customer*   _____ *A stranger*

10 Write About It

A Look at Juanita's message asking for help.
Then look at Ricky's reply.

> Dear Ricky,
> Could you do me a favor? I won't be
> in class tomorrow because I have
> to see the doctor. Could you please
> take notes for me?
> Juanita

B On a piece of paper,
write a message requesting help
from someone in the class.

> Dear Juanita,
> I'm sorry, but I won't be able to
> take notes for you tomorrow. I'm
> not going to school either—I have
> an important singing audition.
> Ricky

C Exchange requests.
Write a reply, accepting or
rejecting the request.

Find the answers to the questions while you read.

1. What was the name of the little boy? _____
2. Who did a favor for him? _____
3. What was the favor? _____
4. What did the boy do with the money? _____
5. What was the boy proud about? _____
6. Why did he write the letter? _____

Dear Sir,

Thirty years ago, I walked into your bakery and asked for some loaves of bread to sell. At the time I was twelve years old. A young lady was working that day. She gave me five loaves and wished me good luck.

I took the loaves and went out to sell them. It took me all day, but I sold every one. At the end of the day, I had more money than I'd ever had before. I was the happiest boy in the world as I walked home that evening.

The next day, I went to a bicycle shop. I paid a deposit on a brand new bicycle. And then I started my next job—as a newspaper delivery boy. Soon I had enough money to complete the payments, and the bike was mine. I was so proud!

Today, I still work in the delivery business. I have a fleet of trucks which deliver goods all over Europe. I live in a beautiful house, but I don't ride a bicycle these days—I drive a large and comfortable car.

I do not know who that young lady was. But because of the start she gave me, I have become a successful man. I'd like to thank her from the bottom of my heart.

Yours sincerely,

George Jenkins

George Jenkins
Durham, England

*T*alk About It

- What is the first job you ever had? What was the pay like?
- Have you ever worked really hard to reach a goal? What was it?
- Talk about a favor that someone did for you. How did you thank the person?

12 Review

1 Vocabulary Review

A Fill in the chart with phrases that go with the verbs you learned in this unit.

Verb	Phrase
type	my presentation
make	
carry	
study	
practice	
take out	
feed	
cook	

B How many ways did you learn to say *Thank you* and *You're welcome* in this unit?

2 Grammar Review

A Make sentences using the words shown.

1. (carry these boxes/meeting room) *Can you help me carry these boxes to the meeting room?*
2. (push my car/gas station) _____
3. (give these copies/sales manager) _____
4. (take this film/photo lab) _____
5. (return these books/library) _____

B Your friend is carrying a big box. She can't open the door to the classroom. You offer to help her. Write the conversation.

You: Do you need some help?

Your friend: _____

You: _____

Your friend: _____

You: _____

3 Log On

Practice more with the language and topics you studied on the *Expressions* website:

http://expressions.heinle.com

Goals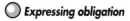

○ *Asking about plans* ○ *Expressing obligation* ○ *Making reservations*

Are you looking forward to your trip?

1 Get Ready

A Look at the activities and the ads. Where can you do each of the activities? Write the number of the activity next to the correct ad (1–4).

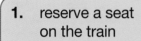

1. reserve a seat on the train
2. make a flight reservation
3. reserve a hotel room
4. reserve a seat on the bus

Sprinter Lines
First In Comfort, First In Safety
1-800-777-2525 for schedule and reservations

Fast Tracks
See The Country By Rail
Call 1-800-936-FAST for ticketing

Spencer Court
In The Heart Of Boston's Historical District
Tel: (617) 555-1000

East Coast Airline
serving more than 80 destinations in the US and Canada for less $
For reservations and info dial 1-888-FLY EAST

B Look at the types of transportation above. How often do you take them? Which do you like best? Why?

2 Start Talking

A Look at the conversation and listen.

Benny: Are you looking forward to your trip?
Ron: Yes, I can't wait.
Benny: Did you reserve a seat on the train?
Ron: Not yet. Do I have to make a reservation?
Benny: You don't have to, but you probably should.
Ron: OK. I'll call the ticket office this afternoon.

Pair work **B** Practice the conversation with a partner. Then practice again using the other information in Get Ready.

3 Listen In

(A) Look at the following items. Check (✔) the ones you usually have to reserve in advance.

_____ *bus*   _____ *subway*   _____ *flight*
_____ *train*   _____ *rental car*   _____ *hotel*

(B) Listen. What are the people reserving? Fill in the first column.

Reserving what?	Where?	When?
1.		
2.		
3.		
4.		

(C) Listen again and fill in *Where?* and *When?*

Try this

There is a longer way to say *May I help you?* What is it? Can you remember?

Are you looking forward to your trip?

Yes. I'm staying at a very fancy hotel.

4 Say It Right

(A) Listen and mark the rising (↗) and falling (↘) intonation, following the example.

1. There's a train at 8:00 __↗__ and one at 10:00 __↘__ .
2. There are buses at 2:30 _____, 4:30 _____ and 7:00 _____.
3. You can reserve a single _____, double _____ or superior _____ room.
4. Would you prefer smoking _____ or non-smoking _____?
5. Do you want economy _____, business _____ or first _____ class?

(B) Listen again and practice.

5 Focus In

(A) **Look at the chart.**

Have to and should	
Do I **have to** make a reservation?	Yes, you do./No, you don't. You don't **have to**, but you probably **should**. You **should** call them at least a day ahead.
Should I take my laptop on vacation?	Yes, you **should**. You might want to check email. No, you **shouldn't**. Just relax and have a good time.

(B) **Look at these travel tips.**
Rewrite the statements using *have to*, *don't have to*, *should* or *shouldn't*.

1. It's a good idea to take a sweater if you're going to England.
_____

2. It isn't necessary to get a visa.
_____

3. In most airports, you must check in more than one hour before your flight.
_____

4. It's not a good idea to take a lot of cash when you go abroad.
_____

(C) **Complete these statements. Then share your ideas with a partner.**

When you go abroad, you…

1. should _____.
2. shouldn't _____.
3. have to _____.
4. don't have to _____.

6 Talk Some More

(A) **Fill in the missing information.**

Agent: Fast Tracks Ticketing. _____ you?

Ron: Yes. _____ any trains to Boston tomorrow morning?

Agent: Yes, there's one at 9:30 and one at 11:00.

Ron: OK. _____ to reserve a seat on the 9:30 train, please.

Agent: _____. Can I have your name, please?

Ron: Sure.

(B) **Check your answers.**

(C) **Next, decide how to continue the conversation and practice it with a partner.**
Then practice again using different forms of transportation and different times.

Fast Tracks Ticketing Office

Work In Pairs   Student A

Student B: Use page 68

A You want to make a flight reservation. You phone the airline. Who speaks first?
What does that person say? Check (✔) the best choice.

_____ Are you calling East Coast Airlines?

_____ East Coast Airlines. May I help you?

_____ Hello. I'm working for East Coast Airlines.

_____ Yes? What do you want?

B Imagine you want to go from New York to Washington.
Call your partner and do the following:

> • *make a flight reservation*
> • *reserve a hotel room*

Fill in the information
your partner gives you.

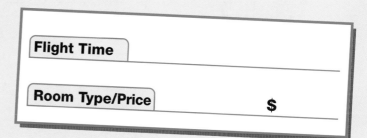

Flight Time _____

Room Type/Price $ _____

C Your partner also needs to make some reservations.
Answer your partner's calls using the following information.

Sprinter Busline
SCHEDULE
Washington, D.C. to New York, N.Y.

DEPARTURE	ARRIVAL
07:00	14:00
09:30	16:30
14:30	21:30
19:00	02:00

ADAMS CAPITOL INN
523 WEST 21ST STREET NEW YORK, N.Y. 10015

Single	$79
Double	$89
Superior	$129

I'd like to make a reservation, please.

Try this

Change roles. Turn to page 68. Do the exercise again using different
times and prices.

Are you looking forward to your trip?

Work In Pairs — Student B

A) You want to make a bus reservation. You phone the bus company.
Who speaks first? What does that person say? Check (✔) the best choice.

_____ Sprinter Busline. Who are you?

_____ You have reached Sprinter Busline.

_____ Thank you for calling Sprinter Busline. How can I help you?

_____ Sprinter. Do you want a bus?

B) Your partner needs to make some reservations.
Answer your partner's calls using the following information.

East Coast Airline

SCHEDULE

New York, N.Y. to Washington, D.C.

DEPARTURE	ARRIVAL
06:30	07:40
10:00	11:10
16:45	17:55
21:15	22:25

Bradstreet Hotel
1550 Bradstreet Avenue W. Washington, D.C. 20013

Single	$85
Double	$99
Superior	$139

I'd like to make a reservation, please.

C) Imagine you want to go from Washington to New York.
Call your partner and do the following:

- *make a bus reservation*
- *reserve a hotel room*

Fill in the information
your partner gives you.

Flight Time	
Room Type/Price	$

Try this

Change roles. Turn to page 67. Do the exercise again using different times and prices.

Express Yourself

 A Work with a partner. Decide a place to go on vacation.
What types of reservations do you have to make? Fill in the chart.

Destination	Reservations

B Practice making the phone reservations with your partner.

C Work with a different person.
Ask about your new partner's travel plans.

Are you looking forward to your trip?

 Think About It

Calling up to make reservations can take a long time, depending on how long you have to wait on the phone. Nowadays, many people make their reservations on the Internet.

- *How about in your country? Do people make reservations on the Internet? What kinds?*
- *Do you use the Internet to make reservations? Why or why not?*

10 **Write About It**

A Look at the description in the travel brochure.

Visit Beautiful Hong Kong

When you visit Hong Kong, you should make reservations well in advance. It's a very popular place, and airlines and hotels are always heavily booked. Chek Lap Kok airport is on a distant island, so when you arrive, you should buy a ticket for the Airport Express train. This will take you to the heart of the downtown district in only 24 minutes.

B Write a brochure describing things people should and shouldn't do when they visit your country.

11 Read On — Accidental Travelers

• *Strategy: Scanning*

Look through the article and find the answers. Which story (1–3) mentions...

1. the island of Guam?   _3_
2. an animal that ate cocoa beans?   _____
3. a surprised truck driver?   _____

4. a trip from West Africa?   _____
5. a very dirty little cat?   _____
6. an animal that eats birds?   _____

Have you ever taken an unexpected trip? Here are three stories of animals that didn't plan on traveling...

2. Hitching a Ride

A Canadian man drove his truck for over 400 kilometers. Then he discovered something very surprising. It was a little cat holding on underneath the truck. He took it to an animal hospital, where the doctor had to give it 16 baths. The doctor decided to keep it and named it Slick. She gave it a good home.

1. Atlantic Stowaway

A ship traveled from West Africa to North America carrying cocoa beans. When workers unloaded the ship, they discovered a small dog. It was very thin and almost dead. For 21 days it had drunk very little water and eaten only cocoa beans. A man took the little dog home with him. He named it Congo. He gave it special care, and soon it was well again.

3. Unwelcome Visitors

Some animal travelers aren't welcome. After World War II, brown tree snakes traveled to Guam on U.S. Navy ships. They had no natural enemies there, so they made themselves at home. They ate the native birds. Since then, the snakes have completely killed five kinds of birds on Guam.

Talk About It

- Do you have any pets? What kind? What are their names?
- What are the most popular pets in your country?
- Have you ever discovered an animal in an unexpected place? Talk about it.

70   Unit 8

12 Review

1 Vocabulary Review

A Fill in the chart with the travel vocabulary you learned in this unit.

Bus	Plane	Train	Hotel

B Which forms of transportation have you used this year?

I'd like to make a reservation, please.

Sorry, we're fully booked.

2 Grammar Review

A Make questions and answers using the words shown.

1. (make/reservation)   *Do I have to make a reservation? No, but you should.*
2. (buy/phrasebook)
3. (get/travel insurance)
4. (check in/early)
5. (wear/seatbelt during flight)

B What should you do if you want to learn to speak English well? Write four sentences using *should*.

1. _____
2. _____
3. _____
4. _____

3 Log On

Practice more with the language and topics you studied on the *Expressions* website:

http://expressions.heinle.com

Goals
○ Offering help   ○ Asking for and giving directions

Turn left on Denver Street.

1 Get Ready

A Where would you go to do the following things? Write the number of the errand in the correct place on the map.

1. cash a check
2. buy some aspirin
3. get the latest novel
4. see a doctor
5. send a package
6. fill your car with gas

B What else can you do at these places? Make a list with a partner.

Other activities

2 Start Talking

A Look at the conversation and listen.

Clerk: Can I help you, sir?
Craig: Yes. Can you tell me how to get to the Central Post Office?
Clerk: Sure. Just go straight. Turn left on Denver Street. You'll see it on the left.
Craig: On Denver Street?
Clerk: Yes, that's right.
Craig: Thanks.

Pair work

B Practice the conversation with a partner.
Then practice again using other places on the map.

3 Listen In

A Where is it? Write the letter of each place next to the clue. One place is extra.

a. medical center
b. movie theater
c. music store
d. post office
e. hotel

1. _____ *Murder at Midnight* is playing here.
2. _____ There are bedrooms, a pool and a business center here.
3. _____ Doctors and nurses work here.
4. _____ From classical music to rock, it's all here.

B Listen and check (✔) the numbers of the conversations where you hear the following expressions (1–4).

	1	2	3	4
tell me how to get to				
I'm looking for				
go straight				
turn right				
turn left				
on the right				
on the left				

C Listen again and number the places the people are looking for (1–4).

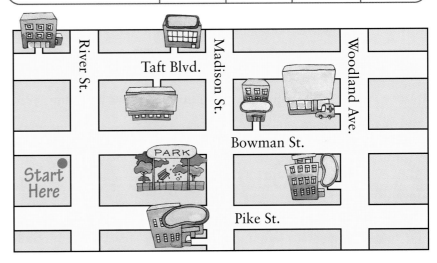

4 Say It Right

A Listen and check (✔) the address you hear.

1. _____ 538 Sheffield Ave.   _____ 5308 Sheffield Ave.
2. _____ 120 Island Rd.   _____ 1210 Island Rd.
3. _____ 836 Lincoln St.   _____ 8136 Lincoln St.
4. _____ 1440 Lakeshore Blvd. _____ 4014 Lakeshore Blvd.
5. _____ 519 Woodland Dr.   _____ 590 Woodland Dr.

Try this
Write down four addresses. Say the addresses to a partner. Your partner will write them down. Was your partner correct?

B Listen again and practice.

Turn left on Denver Street.

5 Focus In

(A) Look at the chart.

Prepositions of location		
How do I get to the bank?	Go straight	**on** this street.
		up/down this street.
	Turn left/right	**at** the gas station.
		at the corner of Wilson Ave. and Denver St.
		on Denver St.
	You'll see it	**on** the left.
	It's there	**on** your right.

(B) Look at the map in Get Ready. Number the instructions from the hotel clerk in the correct order.

_____ Turn right on Denver Street.   _____ Turn left. Go straight on Amber Avenue.

_____ Turn right on Milton Street.   _____ Go up Wilson Avenue until you

_____ You'll see the bank on the right.   come to the intersection.

(C) Fill in the blanks with correct prepositions. Then look at the map in Get Ready. Where does the person want to go? (He is now at the hotel.)

Go straight _____ Wilson Avenue. Turn right _____ the corner of Wilson and

Milton. _____ the gas station, turn left. You'll soon see a bookstore _____

your right. Keep walking for about a minute. You'll see it _____ your left.

6 Talk Some More

(A) Number the sentences to make a conversation (1–7).

Elaine: _____ Where's that?

Elaine: _____ All right. Thank you very much.

Ben: _____ Just walk straight. Turn left on Denver Street. You'll see it on the right.

Ben: ___1___ Can I help you, ma'am?

Elaine: _____ Yes, thank you. I need to cash a check.

Ben: _____ You're welcome.

Ben: _____ Oh, you can cash a check at the First Trust Bank.

> **Spotlight**
> If you don't understand the first time, say:
> *Sorry. Could you say that again, please?*

(B) Check your answers.

**(C) Practice the conversation with a partner.
Then practice again using different places on the map in Get Ready.**

Work In Pairs Student A

A You're at the Ritz Hotel. You're looking for somewhere to do these things. What kind of place would you go to...

- • **eat Italian food?**
- • **watch a movie?**
- • **buy a magazine?**
- • **get traveler's checks?**

B Tell your partner the four things you want to do. Ask for directions. Mark the places on your map.

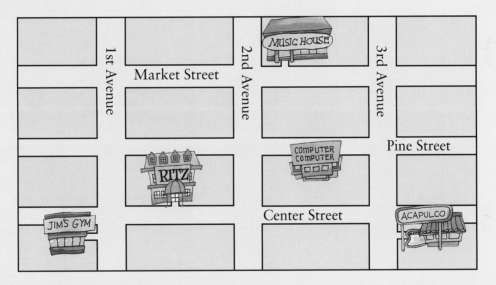

C Listen to your partner's questions. Give your partner directions using your map.

I want to see the dinosaur exhibit.

It's at the Museum of Natural History.

Try this

Put two more public buildings on your map.
Take turns giving directions and marking the new places on your map.

Turn left on Denver Street.

Work In Pairs — Student B

A You're at the Ritz Hotel. You're looking for somewhere to do the following things. What kind of place would you go to...

- • eat Mexican food?
- • buy a CD?
- • work out?
- • buy a printer cable?

B Listen to your partner's questions. Give your partner directions using your map.

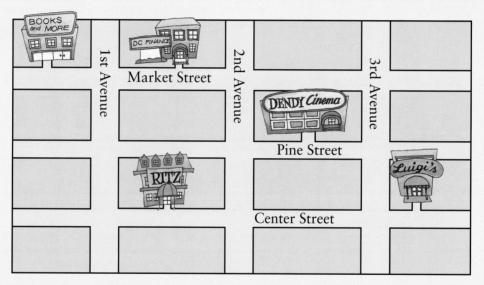

C Tell your partner the four things you want to do. Ask for directions. Mark the places on your map.

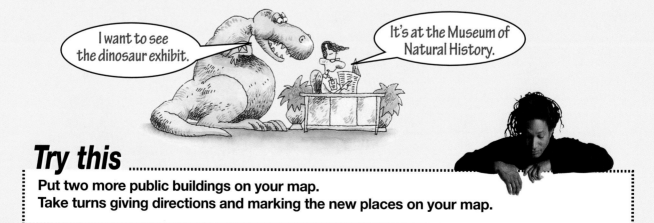

I want to see the dinosaur exhibit.

It's at the Museum of Natural History.

Try this

Put two more public buildings on your map.
Take turns giving directions and marking the new places on your map.

Express Yourself

(A) Write down three errands you need to do.

1. _____
2. _____
3. _____

 Group work

(B) Tell three classmates what you need to do.
Find out a place to do each errand
and how to get there.
Note the information in the chart.

Place	Directions
1. _____	_____
2. _____	_____
3. _____	_____

Think About It

Signs are an important part of communication.
Many signs are similar around the world.
Some are very different.

• *What do you think these signs mean? Do you have similar signs in your country?*

Write About It

(A) Look at the note.

My apartment is pretty easy to find. From the school, take bus number 60 to Burlington Square. Then, walk straight on Benson Avenue about 2 minutes. Turn left at the gas station, and walk straight on Fairlawn Street. The apartment is on the left. Just take the elevator to the fifth floor. I'm in apartment 507.

(B) Write a note to a friend describing how to get from the school to your home.

Turn left on Denver Street.

11 Read On | Maps Don't Help Here

• Strategy: Identifying reference words

Do you think you have a good sense of direction? Come to Fez and test yourself!

The most popular tourist attraction in Fez, Morocco, is the city's oldest section, called the medina. Everyone wants to see the historical buildings and the thousands of little shops. But the medina is perhaps the most confusing place on earth. Maps are useless there.

What makes it so confusing? The streets are very narrow, and they aren't straight. Wherever you walk, you are always turning corners. It's like an unplanned journey into the past. You never know what you will find. That's why people like the medina.

The medina occupies about 10 square kilometers, and around 200,000 people live inside it. There are more than 30,000 homes and over 10,000 small businesses. It's enclosed by city walls that were built hundreds of years ago.

View of the medina from a rooftop in Fez

There *is* a logic to the medina, however. Each product has its own area. The silk merchants are here. The slipper sellers, there. Further on, you can find cotton fabrics. And so on—wool, leather, pottery, woodwork, ironwork...it's all there. And to the local people, it all makes sense.

There are maps of the area, but they aren't very useful. Some visitors have tried using a compass, but it doesn't help either. A guide is your only hope.

Identify the following reference words from the reading.

1. What makes *it* so confusing? (Paragraph 2) **It means** _____.

2. And *they* aren't straight. (Paragraph 2) **They means** _____.

3. *It's* like an unplanned journey into the past. (Paragraph 2) **It means** _____.

4. There are maps of the area, but *they* aren't very useful. (Paragraph 5) **They means** _____.

5. Some visitors have tried using a compass, but *it* doesn't help either. (Paragraph 5) **It means** _____.

Talk About It

○ What's the most confusing place you've ever visited? What made it confusing?

○ Have you ever gotten lost? What happened?

○ If you need directions, do you usually ask someone? Why or why not?

12 Review

1 Vocabulary Review

A Fill in the chart with buildings you learned in this unit.

Places which sell things	Places which offer services

B Choose one of the places in the chart that is near your school.
Give a partner directions to get there.

Can you tell me how to get to the supermarket?

Sure. Go straight on Pine Street...

2 Grammar Review

A Unscramble the sentences.

1. how/bookstore/can/to/to/tell/get/you/me/the _____
2. Pine/left/on/turn/Street _____
3. right/intersection/at/turn/the _____
4. down/First/walk/Avenue _____
5. on/you'll/left/the/it/see _____

B Look back to Get Ready. Write directions from the hotel to the...

1. bookstore _____
2. sports arena _____
3. university _____
4. drugstore _____

3 Log On

Practice more with the language and topics you studied on the *Expressions* website:

http://expressions.heinle.com

UNIT 10

 **Goals** ···

○ *Discussing personal habits* ○ *Talking about degrees*

I drink too much coffee.

1 Get Ready

A Write the number of the word next to the correct picture.

1.	cans
2.	bags
3.	cups
4.	hours

B What else might you drink from a cup? Or a can? What else might you eat from a bag? Make a list.

A cup of...	**A can of...**	**A bag of...**

2 Start Talking

A Look at the conversation and listen.

Colin: I think I drink too much coffee.
Chris: How much do you drink?
Colin: Five cups a day.
Chris: Oh, that is a lot. I only drink one.

 B Practice the conversation with a partner. Then practice again using the other items in Get Ready.

3 Listen In

(A) Look at the sentences about Joseph and Lisa in 'C' below.
Which words do you think are missing?

(B) Listen and write *Lisa* or *Joseph* next to
the correct information.

1. _____ goes to bed at 1:00 a.m.
2. _____ drinks 2 cups of coffee in the evening.
3. _____ drinks 6 cans of soda a day.
4. _____ studies French at 6:30 a.m.
5. _____ gets up at 7:30 a.m.

(C) Listen again and fill in the missing information about Lisa and Joseph.

1. Joseph wants to _____ more, but he can't.
   He thinks it's because he drinks _____ coffee in the evening.
2. Lisa thinks she drinks too much _____ at the office.
   She doesn't drink enough _____.
3. Joseph thinks Lisa's French course starts too early in the _____.
4. Lisa doesn't sleep _____.
   She always wakes up _____ early.

Try this
**How does Joseph say
1:00 a.m.? Can you
remember?**

4 Say It Right

(A) Listen to the example.

Example: He drinks two cups of coffee a day.

(B) Listen and check (✔) the sentences that have the same stress
and rhythm as the example.

1. She drinks three cans of soda a day. _____
2. They eat four bags of candy a day. _____
3. He watches two hours of TV a day. _____
4. She wears two pairs of earrings a night. _____
5. She buys one roll of film a month. _____

Try this
**Write two more sentences
using your own information.
Practice saying them with
the same stress and rhythm
as the example.**

(C) Listen again and practice.

5 Focus In

A Look at the chart.

How much/how many/how often and too/enough		
I drink **too much** soda.	**How much** do you drink?	Five cans a day.
I eat **too many** cakes.	**How many** do you eat?	One a day.
I don't exercise **enough**.	**How often** do you work out?	Once a week.
		Once a month.

B Match the statements with the questions to make three conversations. Draw lines. Then practice them with a partner.

1. I ate too many candy bars.　　How often do you practice?　　Five cups a day.
2. I drink too much coffee.　　How many did you eat?　　Once a week.
3. I don't practice English enough.　　How much do you drink?　　Twelve.

C Match the beginnings of the questions with the correct endings. (There are two answers for each.) Then ask a partner the questions.

1. How much　　_____ English classes do you have?
2. How often　　___1___ money is in your wallet?
3. How many　　_____ do you wash your hair?
　　　　　　　　_____ do you read an evening paper?
　　　　　　　　_____ books are in your bag?
　　　　　　　　_____ TV do you watch?

6 Talk Some More

A Write the words in the correct spaces.

Jenny: I want to play tennis _____.
Billie: Oh? _____ often do you practice?
Jenny: About once a _____.
Billie: Maybe that's not _____.
　　　　I practice about three _____ a week.
Jenny: Really? That's too _____ for me!

 enough　times　better

 much　month　how

B Check your answers.

C Practice the conversation with a partner. Use your own information.

Work In Pairs — Student A

A Fill in the missing information.

speak   meet   play

drink   watch

1. I think I _____ too much soda.
2. I think I _____ too much TV.
3. I want to _____ Spanish better.
4. I want to _____ the piano better.
5. I want to _____ more people.

B Read the sentences above to your partner. Then answer your partner's questions.

C Listen to your partner's information.
Ask questions using the words below.
Note down the information you find out.

eat   drink   go to museums

practice   study

How much do you...?

How often do you...?

I study English three hours a day. How much do you study?

Try this

Think of something you'd like to do better. Tell your partner about it and ask for advice.
Write down your partner's advice.

_____

_____

I drink too much coffee.

Work In Pairs Student B

A Fill in the missing information.

speak   eat   play

drink   learn

1. I think I _____ too much junk food.
2. I think I _____ too much tea.
3. I want to _____ French better.
4. I want to _____ basketball better.
5. I want to _____ more about art.

B Listen to your partner's information. Ask questions using the words below. Note down the information you find out.

practice   study   go to parties

drink   watch

How much do you...?

How often do you...?

C Read the sentences in 'A' above to your partner. Then answer your partner's questions.

I study English three hours a day. How much do you study?

Try this

Think of something you'd like to do better. Tell your partner about it and ask for advice. Write down your partner's advice.

_____

_____

Express Yourself

How often do you practice?

A List two of your good habits and two of your bad habits.

Good habits	Bad habits

Group work **B** Survey three classmates. Complete the chart.
Do they do the same things as you? How much or how often?

	Student 1	Student 2	Student 3
Good habits			
Bad habits			

 Think About It

Many people around the world make New Year's resolutions. These are promises that you make to yourself. Usually you promise to be a better person in the new year. People promise that they will quit smoking, get a new job, take more exercise, and so on.

- *Are New Year's resolutions common in your culture? Have you ever made any? Did you keep them?*

 Write About It

A Look at this letter to an advice column in a magazine.

Dear Dr. Jean,
I'm worried about my sister. She's 22 years old. She drinks six cans of soda a day, and eats five bags of popcorn. She never does any exercise, and spends most of her evenings watching television. What do you think I should tell her?
—Worried Sister

Dear Worried Sister,
Thank you for your letter. I think your sister should...

B Write a reply to the letter.
Then exchange letters. Who has the best advice?

How I Broke a Bad Habit

• *Strategy: Inferring content*

What's the best way to break a bad habit?

Rosely DaSilva, Brazil
My bad habit was biting my fingernails. I did it when I was nervous or when they were a little rough. They looked terrible. I was embarrassed for anyone to see them. Finally, I started carrying a nail file with me. Instead of biting my nails, I began to take care of them. Within a month they looked better.

Grant Wallace, New Zealand
Credit card spending almost ruined my life. My bills were terrible. So I told my older brother about it. He told me to throw away my credit cards. I got a part-time job, and the money goes to my bills. Every week I show my brother the bills and a list of my spending. At the end of the year all the bills will be paid. I'll never lose control of my spending again.

Berta Siswando, Indonesia
I had a habit of eating too much. I always told myself, "Just this once it won't hurt." But I always did it. So I began to lose weight with my best friend. We encourage each other. We keep a list of what we eat, and we show it to each other. When we get really hungry, we take a walk together. The exercise helps, too. After four months we can really see a difference.

Which person might give this advice? (There might be more than one answer.)

1. Find a partner who wants to break the same habit. _____

2. Make a list of what you do. _____

3. Get advice from a family member. _____

4. Do something different instead of the bad habit. _____

5. Notice your progress and be happy about it. _____

---

*T*alk About It

○ Can you think of any more common bad habits?

○ Can you think of any advice for breaking these bad habits?

○ Do you know anyone who has broken a bad habit? How did he or she do it?

12 Review

1 Vocabulary Review

(A) Fill in the chart with expressions you learned in this unit.

Good habits	Bad habits

(B) Can you add any more?

I want to play the violin better.

How often do you practice?

2 Grammar Review

(A) Make sentences using the words shown.

1. John/much/coffee   _John drinks too much coffee._
2. Lisa/many/movies
3. Alice/much/candy
4. Harry/much/TV
5. Gerry/not/sleep/enough

(B) Answer the questions using your own information. How often do you…

1. brush your teeth?
2. watch a movie in English?
3. eat in a restaurant?
4. visit the *Expressions* website?
5. read a magazine in English?
6. talk with a native English speaker?

3 Log On

Practice more with the language and topics you studied on the *Expressions* website:

http://expressions.heinle.com

I drink too much coffee.

87

Goals ⟳ Talking about past events ⟳ Expressing surprise ⟳ Offering congratulations

Did you hear about Laura?

1 Get Ready

A Write the number of the sentence next to the correct picture (1–6).

1. Brian Kim won a trip to London.
2. Laura Austin got married.
3. Richard Steiner's basketball team won their big game.
4. Rita Cruz got a new job.
5. Tom Tang got accepted to Harvard.
6. Jenny Greene had a baby.

B Write down three good things that happened to you recently.

2 Start Talking

A Look at the conversation and listen.

Karen: Did you hear about Laura Austin?
Bessie: No, what happened?
Karen: She got married last week.
Bessie: That's great. Where did you hear that?
Karen: A friend of mine told me.

Pair work **B** Practice the conversation with a partner.
Then practice again using the information about the other people in Get Ready.

3 Listen In

(A) Read the sentences. Write **T** for true, **F** for false. Check with a partner.

1. _____ *That's wonderful!* is the same as *That's great!*

2. _____ *Congratulations!* is always plural.

3. _____ *Really?* is only used in formal situations.

4. _____ *You're kidding!* is the same as *You're joking!*

(B) Listen and check (✔) the numbers of the conversations where you hear these expressions (1–4).

	No. 1	No. 2	No. 3	No. 4
That's great!				
Congratulations!				
Really?				
You're kidding!				

(C) Listen again and number the pictures (1–4).

4 Say It Right

(A) Look at the following expressions of surprise. Mark each one with the correct rising (↗) or falling (↘) intonation.

1. Are you kidding? _____

2. Wow! _____

3. Really? _____

4. That's great! _____

5. I can't believe it! _____

(B) Listen and check your answers.

(C) Listen again and practice.

Try this

Write three sentences describing surprising news. Read them to a partner. Your partner will use intonation to express surprise.

5 Focus In

 A Look at the chart.

get + participle and get + noun phrase			
Did you hear about Kim?	No, what happened?	He **got** She **got**	married. promoted. engaged. his book published. a new job. a pay raise. her driver's license. her MBA.

 B Fill in the blanks to make four conversations.

1. **A:** David and Ann _____ last week.
   B: That's great! When's the wedding?

2. **A:** Did you hear? Kelly _____.
   B: Oh, really? Where is she going to work?

3. **A:** When did you _____?
   B: A month ago, and I love driving.

4. **A:** John finally _____.
   B: He really took a long time to write it!

C Number these six sentences to make a conversation.

___1___ Hello?

_____ Thanks a lot.

_____ I heard you got your MBA.

_____ Hi, Jerry. It's Paula.

_____ Yes, that's right.

_____ That's great news! Congratulations!

6 Talk Some More

A Fill in the missing information.

Brian: Hello?

David: Hi, Brian. It's David. I _____ you _____ a trip to London.

Brian: Yes, that's _____.

David: That's _____ news! I just _____ to call and say congratulations.

Brian: Oh, really? _____ a lot.

won · heard · wanted · thanks · right · great

B Check your answers.

 Pair work **C** Practice the conversation with a partner. Then practice again using the people in Get Ready.

Spotlight

Just is often used to soften a sentence.

Work In Pairs   (Student A)

Student B: Use page 92

A Fill in the information about the four people on the list.
Use your own ideas.

- Paul won _____
- Sara had _____
- Lynn sold _____
- Dennis got _____

> *Did you hear about Louise?*
> *She passed her nursing exam.*
> *No. What happened?*

B Tell your partner about what happened to them.

C Listen to your partner's news and note the information.

Name	What happened?

Try this

Imagine that you have just won a prize. Write what it is on a piece of paper.
Now exchange papers with your partner. Call and congratulate your partner.

Work In Pairs — Student B

Student A: Use page 91

A Fill in the information about the four people on the list. Use your own ideas.

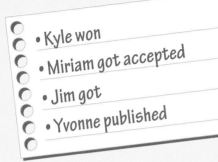

- Kyle won _____
- Miriam got accepted _____
- Jim got _____
- Yvonne published _____

B Listen to your partner's news and note the information.

Name	What happened?

C Tell your partner about what happened to the people in 'A' above.

Did you hear about Louise?

She passed her nursing exam.

No. What happened?

Try this

Imagine that you have just won a prize. Write what it is on a piece of paper. Now exchange papers with your partner. Call and congratulate your partner.

Express Yourself

A Think of a good thing that happened to you recently. Put it on the list.
Now add two more pieces of good news which are not true.

You	Your partner

B Ask your partner questions and note down the information.

Group work **C** Tell other people in your group about your partner's news.
Try to guess which one is true.

What's new?

I won first prize in a baking contest.

Did you hear about Connie? She won...

 Think About It

People offer congratulations in many different ways.
An interesting one is the singing telegram—the person delivering the telegram dresses in a funny costume and sings to the lucky person who receives it.

• *How about in your country? What things do people do to congratulate others?*

Roses are red, violets are blue. You're another year older, and you look like it too!

 Write About It

A Look at the letter.

> Dear Stan,
>
> I just heard you got accepted to Ohio State University.
>
> That's great. Congratulations. I always knew you could do it.
>
> Let's get together and celebrate sometime.
>
> Betsy

B Write a letter to a partner. Congratulate your partner on the good news you heard about in Express Yourself.

• *Strategy: Inferring vocabulary*

Would you like to win a million dollars?

The day she won the lottery was the greatest day of her life. Or so she thought. As she took the check for one million dollars, Val Cratchet started making plans. A new house. A new car. A vacation in the sun. And, of course, she could stop working—give her life a total makeover!

Eight years later, Val was broke. The money was all gone. So were her friends. The new life was over, but how could she go back to her old one?

Winners of sudden wealth often quit their jobs, and then don't know what to do with the time. They may find that close friends grow distant, and that it's difficult to make new ones. The new house in the new surroundings often only leads to more loneliness. What seemed to be wonderful luck turns out to be just the opposite.

It seems that winning a fortune doesn't guarantee happiness. Just ask Val. She now has a new job and new friends but she would probably still say, "Money isn't everything…"

What does each of these words mean?

1. makeover (Paragraph 1)   (a) cleaning   (b) big change   (c) surprise
2. broke (Paragraph 2)   (a) without money   (b) without hope   (c) without friends
3. wealth (Paragraph 3)   (a) money   (b) expensive things   (c) contests
4. surroundings (Paragraph 3)   (a) country   (b) street   (c) neighborhood
5. fortune (Paragraph 4)   (a) lots of money   (b) contest   (c) lottery

---

*T*alk About It

- Do you often enter contests or competitions? What's the best prize you've won?
- What would you do if you won a lot of money?
- There is a saying: *Money can't buy happiness.* Do you think this is true? Why or why not?

12 Review

1 Vocabulary Review

A Fill in the chart with expressions you learned in this unit.

Good things that happen to people	Ways to congratulate people

B Which of the things above have happened to you?

2 Grammar Review

A Complete the sentences with the words shown. Follow the example.

1. (John/get/new job/yesterday)   *John got a new job yesterday.*
2. (Eva/get promoted/last week) _____
3. (Henry/get/driver's license/on Monday) _____
4. (Barb/get engaged/last night) _____

B Your friend David just got accepted to medical school. Write a conversation to congratulate him.

David: Hello?

You: Hi, David, it's _____

_____

David: _____

You: _____

David: _____

3 Log On

Practice more with the language and topics you studied on the *Expressions* website:

http://expressions.heinle.com

I have a terrible headache.

1 Get Ready

A Write the number of the condition next to the correct picture (1–6).

1. headache
2. stuffy nose
3. stomachache
4. fever
5. cough
6. sore throat

B Write a piece of advice for each of these conditions. Choose from the advice below, or make up your own. Compare with a partner.

- *take some aspirin*
  - *drink a lot of juice*
- *go home and rest*
  - *drink some hot tea*
- *take some medicine*
  - *go see a doctor*

1. headache: _____
2. stuffy nose: _____
3. stomachache: _____
4. fever: _____
5. cough: _____
6. sore throat: _____

2 Start Talking

A Look at the conversation and listen.

Jamie: I don't feel very well.

Sue: What's the matter?

Jamie: I have a terrible headache.

Sue: Really? You should take some aspirin.

Jamie: Good idea.

Pair work **B** Practice the conversation with a partner.
Then practice again using the other conditions in Get Ready.

3 Listen In

(A) Look at the four pictures in 'C' below.
What do you think is the matter with these people? Check your ideas with a partner.

(B) Listen and write each person's problem.

	Problem
Shawn	
Linda	
Mary Ann	
Gordon	

(C) Listen again and number the advice that each person is going to follow (1–4).

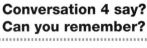

Try this

Instead of *How are you?*, what did Gordon's friend in Conversation 4 say? Can you remember?

4 Say It Right

(A) Listen to the pronunciation of *and* in the sentences below (1–5).

1. I think you should go home and sleep.
2. Drink lots of juice and water.
3. Take some medicine and rest for a while.
4. Drink some hot tea and go to bed.
5. Put a cold towel on your head and lie down.

(B) Listen again and practice.

Try this

Practice the conversations in Start Talking using the advice (1–5). Pay attention to the pronunciation of *and*.

5 Focus In

A Look at the chart.

should and **much/a lot**	
I don't feel well.	You **should** see a doctor.
I have a headache.	I think you **should** take some aspirin.
How are you feeling now?	I feel better now.
	I feel **much** better now.
Is your headache gone?	Yes, I feel **a lot** better now.

B Write advice for someone with these problems.

1. I have a stomachache. _____

2. I have a fever. _____

3. I have a cough. _____

4. I have a headache. _____

C Write complete sentences to make two conversations.

1. **A:** (what/matter)

   _____

   B: (I/terrible/toothache)

   _____

   A: (take/aspirin)

   _____

2. **A:** (how/feeling/now)

   _____

   B: (a lot/better/thanks)

   _____

   A: (glad/hear/it)

   _____

6 Talk Some More

Spotlight

You can use *Glad to hear it* as a response to any kind of good news.

A Number the sentences to make a conversation (1–5).

Jamie: _____ Yes. I took some aspirin. That helped a lot.

Jamie: _____ Much better, thanks.

Sue: _____ Is your headache gone?

Sue: _____ Glad to hear it.

Sue: _____ How are you feeling now?

B Check your answers.

 Pair work

C Practice the conversation with a partner.
Practice again using the other conditions in Get Ready.

Work In Pairs 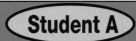 Student A

Student B: Use page 100

A Look at the list of problems in 'B' below. Add two more to the list.

B Tell your partner about your problems. Note the advice your partner gives.

Problem	Advice
headache	
stuffy nose	
sore throat	

C Listen to your partner's problems.
Note the problems, then give your partner advice.

You should eat some chicken soup.

Try this

Imagine one hour has passed. How does your partner feel now? Ask your partner about one of the problems in 'C' above. Then write your conversation below.

You:

Your partner:

You:

Your partner:

You:

Work In Pairs   Student B

A Look at the list of problems in 'C' below. Add two more to the list.

B Listen to your partner's problems.
Note the problems, then give your partner advice.

> You should eat some chicken soup.

C Tell your partner about your problems.
Note the advice your partner gives.

Problem	Advice
cough	
fever	
stomachache	

Try this

Imagine one hour has passed. How does your partner feel now? Ask your partner about one of the problems in 'B' above. Then write your conversation below.

You: _____

Your partner: _____

You: _____

Your partner: _____

You: _____

Express Yourself

A Imagine you're not feeling well. What's the matter? Write down three problems.

My problems	Student 1	Student 2	Student 3

B Ask three classmates for advice.
Note the information in the chart.

 Group work

C Share the advice you received.
Decide who gave the best advice.

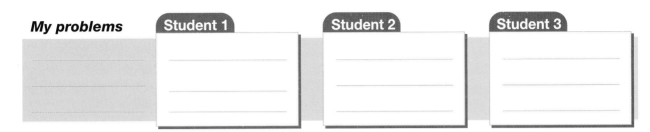 **Think About It**   Many cultures have their own folk remedies for taking care of various conditions. For example, chicken soup is a common treatment for colds in many parts of the world. Although many folk remedies have no scientific proof behind them, many people practice them even today.

• *What folk remedies are popular in your culture? Do you believe in them?*

Write About It

A Look at the get well card.

Dear Josie,
I'm very sorry that you have the flu. Don't worry about things at the office. You should stay home and rest until you feel better.
Take care of yourself!

Glen

B Write a get well card to a friend.
Include at least one piece of advice.

I have a terrible headache.

• *Strategy: Identifying reference words*

Is modern life making some people ill?

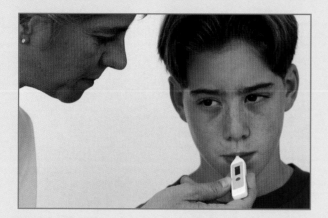

We can be allergic to cats, plants, or to certain foods. But can we be allergic to our environment? Some people think so. They say that chemicals in perfumes and cleaning products can cause allergies. They even think that paints and carpets can make people ill. They call this condition 'environmental illness.'

Doctors disagree about environmental illness. Some doctors believe in it, but other doctors don't. The companies that make perfumes, paints, carpets and cleaners say their products are safe.

The city of Halifax in Nova Scotia, Canada takes environmental illness very seriously. They ask people not to wear perfumes in public places. This includes deodorants and hair care products. These items are not allowed in some schools, offices, hospitals, libraries, or theaters. They are not even allowed on city buses.

Some companies see a good market in environmental illness. They are making special products that are 'safe.' These include cleaners, hair products, carpeting, and building supplies. The products contain no perfumes and no dangerous chemicals.

**Look at these sentences from the reading passage.
What does the reference word mean in each one?**

1. *They* call this condition 'environmental illness.' (Paragraph 1)   *They* means ___some people___

2. Some doctors believe in *it*. (Paragraph 2)   *It* means _____

3. *They* are not even allowed on city buses. (Paragraph 3)   *They* means _____

4. *They* are making special products... (Paragraph 4)   *They* means _____

5. *These* include cleaners… (Paragraph 4)   *These* means _____

Talk About It

○ Do you know someone with an allergy? What are they allergic to?

○ Do you think the environment in your area affects people's health? In what ways?

○ What kinds of things do you think should not be allowed in public places? Why?

Review

1 Vocabulary Review

A Fill in three conditions you learned in this unit.
Then write some remedies for each one.

Conditions	Remedies

B What advice would you
give to someone
with these problems?

What's the matter?

You should go
lie down.

I have
a terrible
headache!

2 Grammar Review

A Number the sentences to make a conversation.

_____ Much better, thanks.

_____ Yes, I drank some hot tea. That helped a lot.

_____ Glad to hear it.

_____ How are you feeling now?

_____ Is your stomachache gone?

B Unscramble the sentences.

1. don't/well/feel/I/very _____

2. terrible/I/a/headache/have _____

3. aspirin/should/an/take/you _____

4. now/feeling/how/you/are _____

5. a/feel/I/lot/thanks/now/better _____

3 Log On

Practice more with the language and topics you studied on the *Expressions* website:

http://expressions.heinle.com

I have a terrible headache.

Goals
● Discussing job experience and education   ● Making comparisons

Do you have any experience?

1 Get Ready

A Look at the resumes. What kind of work experience do these people have? What kind of educational qualifications do they have?

Nancy Maynard
- Sales Representative:
  2 years at Coretel Industries
- BS in Marketing

Helen Garcia
- Assistant Sales Manager
  2 years at Edison Petroleum Company
- Master's Degree in Business Administration

Wilson Koh
Sales Assistant
1 year at Halifax Inc.
Master's Degree in International
Business Administration

Craig Markstein
- Regional Sales Representative:
  1 year at Global Marketing, Inc.
- BS in Accounting

B Look at the job ad. Which person would you choose for the job? Why?

> **BETA LABORATORIES**
> Join a growing sales force and work with the best. Experience necessary. Bring resume detailing work experience and educational history to: *Beta Laboratories, 2983 Santa Mesa Way, Culver City, California*

2 Start Talking

A Look at the conversation and listen.

Mr. Hedges: So, Ms. Maynard, you want to work in sales?
Ms. Maynard: Yes, that's right.
Mr. Hedges: Do you have any experience?
Ms. Maynard: Yes, I do. I worked in the sales department of Coretel Industries for two years.
Mr. Hedges: I see. And what was your major at school?
Ms. Maynard: I studied marketing.
Mr. Hedges: All right. Thank you very much.

Pair work **B** Practice the interview with a partner.
Then practice again using the other people in Get Ready.

3 Listen In

A Look at the job ads in 'C' below. What kinds of jobs are these? How many years' experience do you think a person needs for each one? Compare your ideas with a partner.

B Listen to the interviews and fill in the missing information.

	Experience	Majored in?
Ruth Harrington		journalism
Stephen Adams		business management
Joanna Tate	2 years/shipping clerk	
Richard Foster	none	

C Listen again and number the ads (1–4).

Loan Officer
For Busy Bank

• *Good opportunity*
Call 429-1236 for interview

WANTED!
Night Manager
• Experience needed.
Fairview Hotels, Inc.
939-4398

Ever think about a career in advertising?
Fast-paced firm needs account assistants. Experience not necessary.

Call 558-2138
for interview

Fashion Editor Needed
for Growing Magazine
Experience Preferred
Contact Sally Jameson at 711-1385 for interview

Try this
How do the interviewers say *sit down*? Can you remember?

4 Say It Right

A Look at the words on the left. Write each one under the word with the same stressed syllable.

	can di date	de **part** ment
manager exactly assistant position resume regional accounting interview qualify requirement		

B Listen and check your answers.

C Listen again and practice.

Do you have any experience?   **105**

5 Focus In

A Look at the charts.

more/most
Joe has some experience.
Jenny has **more** experience than Joe.
Stella has **the most** experience in the group.

better/best
Joe's a good person for the job.
Jenny's a **better** person for the job.
Stella's **the best** person for the job.

B Look at the information and fill in the blanks in the sentences.

Name: Gerry Brown **Experience:** 6 months at Flux Industries
Name: Sandy Kwok **Experience:** 1 year at International Manufacturing
Name: Maria Verde **Experience:** 3 years at Global Trade

1. Gerry, Sandy and Maria all have _____ work experience.

2. Sandy has _____ experience _____ Gerry,
   but Maria has _____ experience _____ Sandy.

3. Sandy has _____ experience. She is _____ person for the job.

C Look at the information and read the sentences. Write *T* for true or *F* for false.

	Colin	Chris	David	Sean
Swimming 100m:	1.5 min.	1.26 min.	1.25 min.	1.4 min.
Running 100m:	11 sec.	11.5 sec.	12.1 sec.	13 sec.

1. _____ Colin is the best runner in the group.
2. _____ Sean is a better swimmer than David.
3. _____ Chris is a better runner than David.
4. _____ Colin is a better swimmer than Sean.

6 Talk Some More

A Write the words in the correct places.

most has call
best worked

Ms. DeVille: Who's the_____ person for the sales position?
Mr. Hedges: Well, Helen Garcia has the _____ experience.
   She _____ at Edison Petroleum for two years.
   And she _____ an MBA.
Ms. DeVille: All right. Let's _____ her in
   for a second interview.

Spotlight
MBA stands for Master of
Business Administration.

B Check your answers.

Pair work

C Practice the conversation with a partner. Then practice again using the resumes in Get Ready. Why aren't the other people the best ones for the job?

A What qualifications do you think would be useful to become a bookstore manager? Write them here. Compare your ideas with your partner.

B These four people are all applying for a job as a bookstore manager. Take turns asking about the people. Write the missing information.

Jim Snyder
- Cashier at a bookstore 2 years' experience
- Major: English

Patty Conners

Cynthia Farber

RONALD LYNDQUIST
- Assistant manager/bookstore 1 year
- Major: accounting

WANTED: BABYSITTER

Does he have any experience?

C Check with your partner. Who would you like to call for interview? Discuss who you think is the best candidate.

Try this

Write an interview with your partner. Then role-play the interview with your partner.

7 Work In Pairs (Student B)

A What qualifications do you think would be useful to become a bookstore manager? Write them here. Compare your ideas with your partner.

B These four people are all applying for a job as a bookstore manager. Take turns asking about the people. Write the missing information.

Cynthia Farber
Manager at a clothing store for 2 years
Major: marketing

Patty Conners
• Salesperson at a newsstand for 2 years
• Major: literature

Jim Snyder

RONALD LYNDQUIST

WANTED: BABYSITTER

Does he have any experience?

C Check with your partner.
Who would you like to call for interview?
Discuss who you think is the best candidate.

Try this

Write an interview with your partner. Then role-play the interview with your partner.

8 Express Yourself

(A) Write your resume. It can be real or imaginary.

──────── Resume ────────

Name: _____

Experience: _____

Education: _____

NEEDED IMMEDIATELY!

Word Processing Assistant

Must have computer experience.
Call 433-8793 for details.

 Pair work

(B) Imagine you're applying for one of these jobs. Your partner is applying for the other. Take turns interviewing each other.

 Group work

(C) Compare your partner with other applicants for the job. Who is the best candidate?

─ Popular fast food chain ─
is looking for:

Assistant Managers
*Experience preferred,
but not necessary.*

Call 859-7777
to schedule an interview.

9 Think About It

In most English-speaking countries, some interview questions are not OK. For example, interviewers generally do not ask about age, race or religion. The idea is that employers should be fair and treat all people applying for a job equally.

- *How about in your culture? What questions are OK to ask at interviews? Which ones are not OK?*

10 Write About It

(A) Look at the letter of application.

Personnel Manager
Beta Laboratories
Santa Mesa Way
Culver City, California

July 14

Dear Sir or Madam,

I am writing to apply for the position of sales representative with your company. From my resume, which is attached, you will see that I have all the qualifications you are looking for. I have two years' experience in sales, and I majored in business administration at school. I look forward to hearing from you.

Sincerely,

Dolores Maclaine

Dolores Maclaine

(B) Write an application letter for the job you chose in Express Yourself.

A New Kind of Summer Job

• *Strategy: Scanning*

What kind of jobs do students like to get in the summer?

In many parts of the world, university students work in the summer. They need the money, and they can get some working experience. Traditionally, they get jobs as servers, cashiers, and lifeguards at swimming pools.

These days, however, more and more students are working at *dotcoms*. Dotcoms are Internet-based companies which offer goods and services online. Today's young people already know a lot about computers, and they can quickly learn more. The pay is also usually much better than at the traditional summer jobs.

There are other advantages besides the pay. Students see dotcom jobs as a good start on their future. In addition to good experience, the work is also enjoyable for

most. On top of this, their co-workers treat them with respect.

Dotcoms are new and need new ways of thinking. Imagination and enterprise are more important than formal qualifications. So some students are even quitting school to start their own dotcoms. A recent survey of dotcom executives finds that 2% of them are under 30 years old, and 12% never finished university.

Write the correct paragraph number in the spaces. Which paragraph (1–4) talks about...

1. good pay in dotcom jobs? _____

2. the age of dotcom executives? _____

3. the jobs students used to take in the summer? _____

4. good job experience for students' future careers? _____

5. what *dotcom* means? _____

---

*T*alk About It

○ Have you had part-time or summer jobs? What were they? Did you enjoy them?

○ What kinds of summer jobs are popular for students in your country? Why?

○ Would you like a dotcom job? Why or why not?

12 Review

1 Vocabulary Review

A Fill in the chart with the words you learned in this unit.

Jobs	Majors

B What majors are good to get the jobs above?

Who's the best person for the job?

Don has the most experience.

WANTED:
SWIMMING INSTRUCTOR

2 Grammar Review

A Make sentences. Follow the example.

1. John has 3 years' experience. Mary has 4 years' experience. Tom has 5 years' experience.
Mary has more experience than John, but Tom has the most experience.

2. Patty has $75. Ying Li has $80. Mohammed has $50.

_____

3. Joanna has 100 CDs. Cynthia has 150 CDs. Pascal has 120 CDs.

_____

B Make a conversation using the words shown.

1. who's/best person/job   _____

2. John Garcia/most/experience   _____

3. how much/experience/have   _____

4. worked/Flux Industries/four years _____

5. have/qualifications   _____

6. yes/MBA   _____

3 Log On

Practice more with the language and topics you studied on the *Expressions* website:

http://expressions.heinle.com

Goals

○ *Making plans* ○ *Discussing experience* ○ *Describing places*

Have you been to the new mall?

1 Get Ready

PHOTO EXHIBIT

DJ

food

Swimming Pool

Monkey Exhibit

Women's Shops

A Write the number of the place next to the correct picture (1–6).

> 1. Winfield's Mall
> 2. Amazon Sports Club
> 3. Angelo's Restaurant
> 4. City Zoo
> 5. Galaxy Dance Club
> 6. Museum of Modern Art

B Look at the pictures and fill in the blanks.

1. *The museum:* There's an interesting _photo exhibit_ .
2. *The sports club:* They have a new _____.
3. *The restaurant:* Their _____ is really _____.

4. *The zoo:* There's a new _____.
5. *The dance club:* The DJ is _____.
6. *The mall:* A new _____ just opened.

2 Start Talking

A Look at the conversation and listen.

Marie: Are you doing anything this weekend?
Sandra: No, why?
Marie: Well, have you ever been to the City Zoo?
Sandra: No, I haven't.
Marie: The new monkey exhibit there is really interesting. Would you like to go?
Sandra: All right.

Pair work

B Practice the conversation with a partner.
Then practice again using the other information in Get Ready.

A Have you ever been to any of the places in the chart below? When? Where? Tell a partner.

B Listen and number the places Tim and Angie talk about in the correct order (1–4).

	Has Tim been there?		Has Angie been there?	
☐ museum	yes	no	yes	no
☐ coffee shop	yes	no	yes	no
☐ Indian restaurant	yes	no	yes	no
☐ dance club	yes	no	yes	no

C Have Tim and Angie been to the places? Listen again and circle *yes* or *no*.

Try this

Tim uses another expression for *sounds boring*. Can you remember what it was?

Have you been to the new mall?

No. But I hear it's very crowded.

4 Say It Right

A Sometimes *want to* and *want a* both sound like *wanna*.
Listen to the sentences and check (✔) the correct column.

want to	want a
1.	
2.	
3.	
4.	

Try this

Write four sentences, using *want to* or *want a*. Say your sentences to a partner. Speak as quickly as you can. Your partner will say *want to* or *want a*.

B Listen again and practice.

5 Focus In

A Look at the chart.

Have been	
Have you (ever) **been** to the city zoo?	Yes, I **have**. Yes, I**'ve** already **been** there. No, I **haven't been** there yet. No, I**'ve** never **been** there.

B Fill in the blanks with the correct form of *have* or *have not*.

1. I _____ been to San Francisco, but I'd love to go.
2. No, Gina _____ been to the new mall, but Tony _____.
3. You _____ never been to Paris? You have to go!
4. Yes, Lance _____ been to the Thai restaurant, but he _____ been to the Indian one.
5. We _____ been to the Science Museum once. I'd highly recommend it.

C Unscramble the questions. Then ask your partner.

1. ever/been/Europe/have/you/to _____
2. museum/you/the/ever/local/have/been/to _____
3. have/pet/show/ever/a/been/to/you _____
4. amusement/have/ever/been/to/an/you/park _____

6 Talk Some More

Spotlight
Sounds good. We can also say *looks good*, *smells good*, *tastes good* or *feels good*.

A Write the words in the correct spaces.

Ray: Do you want to go to the new mall this Saturday?

Carl: I've _____ there already. It's kind of _____.

Ray: Oh, really? Well, what do you _____ to do?

Carl: I _____ been to that new sports club yet.

Ray: Do you want to go _____?

Carl: _____ good to me.

been   there   sounds

want   boring   haven't

B Check your answers.

Pair work **C** Practice the conversation with a partner. Use your own information, or talk about the other places in Get Ready.

Work In Pairs Student A

A Where do you want to go this weekend? Why do you want to go there?
Fill in the information.

Place	Reason
1.	
2.	

B Have you been to any of these?
Check (✔) the ones you've been to.

	You	Your Partner
• **a baseball game**		
• **a French restaurant**		
• **an opera**		
• **a zoo**		
• **a cybercafé**		

C Ask questions and find out which ones your partner has been to.
Check (✔) those places in the chart. Then answer your partner's questions.

Have you been to the new shoe store yet?

No. What's it like?

It's really nice. You should go.

Maybe I'll go this weekend.

Try this

Do the exercise again using the places you wrote about in 'A' above. Then decide to go to two places together. Choose one from each list. Write your reasons below.

_____

_____

_____

Work In Pairs — Student B

A Where do you want to go this weekend? Why do you want to go there?
Fill in the information.

Place	Reason
1.	
2.	

B Have you been to any of these?
Check (✔) the ones you've been to.

	You	Your Partner
• *a basketball game*		
• *a vegetarian restaurant*		
• *a photo exhibit*		
• *a history lecture*		
• *a jazz concert*		

C Answer your partner's questions. Then ask questions about the list above and find out which ones your partner has been to. Check (✔) those places in the chart.

Have you been to the new shoe store yet?

It's really nice. You should go.

No. What's it like?

Maybe I'll go this weekend.

Try this

Do the exercise again using the places you wrote about in 'A' above. Then decide to go to two places together. Choose one from each list. Write your reasons below.

_____

_____

_____

Express Yourself

A List five places in your city that you think are interesting.

Place	Person
1.	
2.	
3.	
4.	
5.	

B Survey several classmates. Find a person who has never been to each place. Invite the person to go there. Write a different name for each place on the list.

Group work **C** Find one place that no one in the group has been to, but everyone would like to visit.

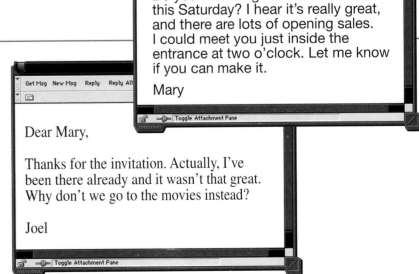

I would never try that!

Think About It

People around the world are constantly searching for new, exciting experiences. That's the reason why activities like snowboarding and bungee jumping have become so popular in recent years.

* *What kinds of exciting sports are popular in your country? Have you ever tried any of them?*

Write About It

A Look at the email messages.

Get Msg New Msg Reply Reply All Forward File Next Print Delete Stop

Hi Joel,

Do you want to go to the new mall this Saturday? I hear it's really great, and there are lots of opening sales. I could meet you just inside the entrance at two o'clock. Let me know if you can make it.

Mary

Toggle Attachment Pane

Get Msg New Msg Reply Reply All

Dear Mary,

Thanks for the invitation. Actually, I've been there already and it wasn't that great. Why don't we go to the movies instead?

Joel

Toggle Attachment Pane

B Write an email message to a friend inviting him or her to join you on the weekend. Then exchange messages and write a reply.

Have you been to the new mall?

• *Strategy: Scanning*

Fill in the chart with information about the two skating events.

	Sunday afternoon	Friday night
1. Who does it?		
2. Where do they do it?		
3. When do they do it?		
4. How do they do it?		

Planning a trip to Paris? Don't forget to pack your inline skates!

What's the best way to tour Paris? Not everyone takes a tour bus or a taxi. Some people put on their skates to see the city. There are two special events.

Courtesy of Reuters/Gareth Watkins

You might want to start with the Sunday afternoon event. You join thousands of other skaters in a group that's two kilometers long. You pass all of the famous sights of Paris. You skate along a route that is closed to cars. The skaters are mostly in their 20s and 30s, but there are many small children and quite a few older people. The speed is slow and comfortable.

But there's another event—if you are good enough. It's called 'Friday Night Fever' and it's 25 kilometers long. Paris looks even more exciting by night, when you are skating fast. From 10:00 p.m. until 1:00 a.m., thousands of skaters whiz down a special route. Police officers on motorbikes lead the way.

The lead skaters are fast and brave. They sometimes jump over the hoods of parked cars. Some skaters play drums, and others carry large stereos.

Talk About It

◯ Do you see a lot of inline skaters in your city? How old are they? Have you ever tried it?

◯ Have you ever been in or watched a race? What kind was it?

◯ Think of something you've always wanted to try. Why haven't you tried it yet?

1 Vocabulary Review

A Fill in the chart with places you learned in this unit.

Eating places	Entertainment places	Educational places

B Which of these places do you often go to?

Have you ever been to the zoo?

No, I haven't.

2 Grammar Review

A Unscramble these sentences.

1. want/to/evening/out/you/go/this/do _____
2. a/sounds/that/great/like/idea _____
3. to/Thai/been/have/new/the/you/restaurant _____
4. yet/I/no/been/haven't/there _____

B Answer the questions. Write complete sentences.

1. Have you ever been abroad? Where did you go?

_____

2. Have you ever been to a concert? Who did you see?

_____

3. Have you ever been to a big sports event? Who won?

_____

4. Have you ever slept for more than twelve hours? Why were you so tired?

_____

3 Log On

Practice more with the language and topics you studied on the *Expressions* website:

http://expressions.heinle.com

Goals

○ Making recommendations ○ Describing places and objects

I took your advice.

Get Ready

A Look at the pictures. What are the reasons for doing these things? Write the number of the reason next to the correct picture (1–5).

1. I went there last summer. It was really nice.

2. My brother owns one. He said it runs great.

3. I took a class there. I learned a lot about the Internet

4. A friend of mine went there. They have a great homestay program.

5. I'm a member there. They have really good equipment.

Buy a car   Take a trip

Study abroad   Join a health club

Take a computer class

B Make two more recommendations. Give reasons. Then compare your ideas with a partner.

1. **A:** I'm thinking about studying a new language.
   B: _You should_ _____

2. **A:** I'm thinking about buying a computer.
   B: _You should_ _____

Start Talking 📼

A Look at the conversation and listen.

Paul: I'm thinking about taking a trip this summer.
Brenda: Oh, you should go to Boston.
I went there last summer. It was really nice.
Paul: OK. I'll think about it.

Pair work **B** Practice the conversation with a partner. Then practice again using the other information in Get Ready.

3 Listen In

(A) Look at the *Thinking about...* list below. Where would you go if you wanted to do these things? Compare your ideas with a partner.

(B) Match the name with what the person is thinking about doing.

Name	Thinking about...	Reasons
1. Elaine ➤	• taking tennis lessons ➤	• They're having a sale.
	• buying a computer ➤	• It's a beautiful place.
2. Alison ➤	• buying a new house ➤	• The instructors are very good.
	• buying a stereo ➤	• The service is fast.
3. Fred ➤	• taking a trip ➤	• The schedule is convenient.
	• joining a health club ➤	• There's a large selection.
	• taking skiing lessons ➤	• There's a lot to do there.
4. Ben ➤	• moving to a new apartment ➤	• The staff is friendly.

(C) Listen again and match each activity with the two reasons for the recommendations. (You may not hear the exact words.)

Are the instructors good here?

Try this

In the first conversation, you heard a different way to ask *How's it going?* What was it? Can you remember?

4 Say It Right

(A) Listen to the example.

Example: The staff is very friendly.

(B) Listen and check (✔) the sentences that have the same stress and rhythm as the example.

1. _____ They have a large selection.
2. _____ It's a very beautiful place.
3. _____ There is a lot to do there.
4. _____ The instructors are very good.
5. _____ The school is really pretty.

Try this

Look at the sentences you checked. Work with a partner. Use them to make conversations like the one in Start Talking. Practice the conversations.

(C) Listen again and practice.

I took your advice.

5 Focus In

(A) **Look at the chart.**

> **Why and *because***
>
> | | |
> |---|---|
> | **Why** should I go to the Virtual Institute? | **Because** you can learn about the Internet. |
> | **Why** should we move to a new apartment? | **Because** this one is too small. |
> | **Why** should Jennie buy a Land Cruiser? | **Because** they're safe, and they run great. |

(B) **Look at the example.**

Example:
Ally/taking a trip/New England/beautiful place/lots to do.
A: Ally's thinking about taking a trip.
B: She should go to New England.
A: Why should she go there?
B: Because it's a beautiful place and there's a lot to do.

On a piece of paper, write two more conversations. Use the words below.

1. Ben/buying a new car/Al's Garage/good selection
2. Alicia/moving/new house/my neighborhood/it's quiet/has good stores

(C) **Now practice the conversations above with a partner.**

6 Talk Some More

(A) **Fill in the missing information.**

Brenda: _____, Paul. Long time no see.
Paul: Yeah, I took your advice.
I _____ to Boston.
Brenda: Oh, _____? How _____ it?
Paul: Wonderful. I had a great _____.
I'm glad I went.
Brenda: I knew you would _____ it.

(B) **Check your answers.**

(C) **Practice the conversation with a partner.**
Then practice again using the other information in Get Ready.

Work In Pairs

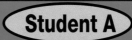
A Look at the places and the reasons in 'C' below. For each one, add one more reason your partner might want to go there.

B Tell your partner you're thinking of doing the following things.
Note your partner's recommendations. Ask for reasons.

I'm thinking about...

taking a painting class
taking a trip
renting a video
going out for dinner

Recommendations

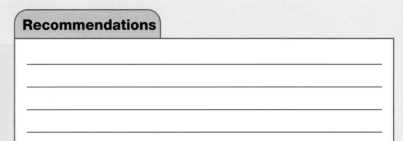

C Listen to your partner and recommend the best places. Give reasons.

Place

TJ Appliance Center
Trustmore Finance
A-1 Language Institute
Fitness World

Reasons for going	
having a sale	
convenient location	
great instructors	
good equipment	

Try this

Imagine one week has passed. You meet your partner again. Tell your partner about the recommendations you followed. What happened? Write it here.

_____

_____

I took your advice.

7 Work In Pairs (Student B)

A Look at the places and the reasons in 'B' below. For each one, add one more reason your partner might want to go there.

B Listen to your partner and recommend the best places. Give reasons.

Place	**Reasons for going**	
Movie Land Videos	big selection	
Miami Beach	beautiful	
Café Lorenza	great food	
Paloma Art Academy	convenient schedule	

I'm thinking of taking skiing lessons.

Why not?

Well, you shouldn't take lessons at Ace Skiing School.

Because that's where I went.

C Tell your partner you're thinking of doing the following things. Note your partner's recommendations. Ask for reasons.

I'm thinking about...	**Recommendations**
joining a health club	
buying a TV	
opening a bank account	
taking an English class	

Try this

Imagine one week has passed. You meet your partner again. Tell your partner about the recommendations you followed. What happened? Write it here.

_____

_____

Express Yourself

A List three things you're thinking about doing this week.

Activity	Recommendation
1.	
2.	
3.	

Group work

B Tell your partners what you're thinking about doing. For each activity, get a recommendation and a reason from three different people. Then write the best recommendations in the chart.

> Recently, I met someone very special, but my problem is that he doesn't like pets very much.

Think About It

In many cultures, people write to newspapers to get advice on problems. Here they can get advice on anything from relationships to jobs to dining etiquette.

- *How about in your culture? Do newspapers have advice columns? What kinds of problems do people need advice on?*

Write About It

A Look at the advertisement.

BOSTON THE BEAUTIFUL!
Why should you visit Boston this summer?

Because...
  ...it's beautiful!
  ...you can learn about America's history!
  ...it has great shopping!
  ...there's so much to see and do!

Come and visit us! Call 1 (800) 555-9389 for information.

Boston Tourism Bureau

B Write an advertisement for your city.
Then exchange advertisements. Who has the most interesting one?

I took your advice.

Read On — Advice Through Proverbs

• *Strategy: Inferring content*

Do you know any English proverbs?

Proverbs are common across most of the world's cultures and languages. These are little sayings that express a wise truth or a piece of advice. Sometimes it's easy to understand their meaning. Other times the meaning is more hidden, or harder to understand. Proverbs from a foreign language can be especially difficult. Here are some very common proverbs in English:

1 *Rome was not built in a day.*

2 *The grass is always greener on the other side.*

3 *Don't cry over spilled milk.*

4 *Don't judge a book by its cover.*

5 *Let sleeping dogs lie.*

6 *Don't count your chickens before they're hatched.*

7 *One man's meat is another man's poison.*

8 *You can lead a horse to water, but you can't make it drink.*

9 *You can't have your cake and eat it too.*

10 *Blood is thicker than water.*

What do you think the proverbs above mean?
Write the number of the proverb with the closest meaning.

a. You can't really know a person by just looking at them. _____

b. Don't spend your money before you have it. _____

c. People always want the things that they don't have. _____

d. If something bad happens, put it behind you. Keep moving forward. _____

e. You can't have everything exactly the way you want it. _____

f. Be patient. Some things can't be done quickly. _____

g. Family members are more important than other people. _____

h. Don't make trouble. _____

i. Not all people like the same things. _____

j. You can't force people to do something if they don't want to do it. _____

Talk About It

O Do you know any other proverbs in English?

O Do you have proverbs in your language that are similar to the ones above?

O What's your favorite proverb in your own language? What does it mean? Can you translate it into English?

12 Review

1 Vocabulary Review

A Unscramble the verbs from this unit.

1. nur _____
2. noji _____
3. pone _____

4. tren _____
5. vome _____

B Write the verbs from 'A' in the spaces.

1. _____ a fitness center
2. _____ a bank account
3. _____ great

4. _____ an apartment
5. _____ house

I'm thinking about taking a vacation.

You should go on a cruise. It's really relaxing.

2 Grammar Review

A What would you recommend to a friend who says the following? Follow the example.

1. I'm thinking about studying English.   *You should try my language school.*
2. I'm thinking about taking a vacation.   _____
3. I'm thinking about buying a car.   _____
4. I'm thinking about going out for dinner.   _____
5. I'm thinking about quitting smoking.   _____

B Now give reasons for your recommendations.

1. *Because the teachers are really great.*
2. _____
3. _____
4. _____
5. _____

3 Log On

Practice more with the language and topics you studied on the *Expressions* website:

http://expressions.heinle.com

I took your advice.

○ *Discussing errands*   ○ *Apologizing*   ○ *Making excuses*

Did you mail those letters?

Get Ready

A Look at the picture. Which items on the list were done today? Check (✔) the pictures.

1. mail letters
2. get groceries
3. return videos
4. pick up medicine at drugstore
5. pick up shirts at dry cleaner's
6. take film in to be developed

B Write two errands that you have to do today or tomorrow.

○
○
○
○

Start Talking

A Look at the conversation and listen.

Jill: Hi, I'm home.

Greg: Oh, hi, dear.

Jill: Did you get the groceries today?

Greg: Yes, I did. Did you mail those letters?

Jill: Sorry, I forgot.

Greg: That's OK.

Jill: I'll do it tomorrow.

Pair work

B Practice the conversation with a partner.
Then practice again using the other errands in the picture, as well as your own.

3 Listen In

A Listen and write each name in the correct place.

(Jonathan)　(Roger)　(Jennifer)　(Tammy)

Name	Errands	Excuse
1. _____	• go to the doctor's • buy a birthday gift	• take boss to the bus station • pick up uncle at the airport
2. _____	• return library books • pay credit card bill	• go to the eye doctor's • pick up VCR at the repair shop
3. _____	• buy milk • call the travel agency	• take computer to be fixed • go to the bookstore
4. _____	• wash the car • pick up the photos	• buy film for the camera • go to a lunch meeting

B Listen and circle the errands that each person *didn't* do.

C Listen again and match the errand that wasn't done with the correct excuse.

Try this

How did Tammy describe her day? Can you remember?

4 Say It Right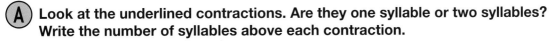

A Look at the underlined contractions. Are they one syllable or two syllables? Write the number of syllables above each contraction.

1. I <u>don't</u> have time to go to the bank today.

2. I <u>didn't</u> take the books back to the library.

3. He <u>wasn't</u> able to get a haircut this afternoon.

4. They <u>weren't</u> able to attend the meeting at 3:00.

5. I <u>couldn't</u> go to the post office because my bus was late.

Try this

How about the words *aren't, mustn't, shouldn't, can't* and *isn't*? One syllable or two? Check your answers with a partner.

B Listen and check your answers.

C Listen again and practice.

5 Focus In

A Look at the chart.

was able to and **had to**	
Did you get the groceries?	Yes, I did. No, I didn't. I **had to** take the car to the garage. Sorry, I forgot.
Were you able to mail the letters?	Yes, I mailed them this morning. No, I **wasn't (able to)**. I **had to** go to a meeting.

B There are four mistakes in the conversation. Underline them.
Then write the corrected form in the space.

Sue: Did you wash the car?   _____

Pete: No, I wasn't.   _____

Sue: And was you able to go to the bank?   _____

Pete: No, I didn't.   _____

Sue: Why not?   _____

Pete: Sorry, I was busy today. I have to work overtime.   _____

C Imagine you were not able to do these errands. Why not? Write excuses.

1. Did you wash the car?   _No, I didn't. I didn't have time._

2. Were you able to mail those letters?   _____

3. Did you go to the bank?   _____

4. Did you buy a birthday gift for your mom?   _____

5. Were you able to call your brother?   _____

6 Talk Some More

(what) (wasn't) (have)

(did) (not) (had)

A Fill in the missing information.

Millie: _____ a busy day!

Joe: Mine was too. _____ you return the videos this afternoon?

Millie: No, I _____ able to.

Joe: Why _____?

Millie: I _____ to take the car to the garage.
I didn't _____ time.

> **Spotlight**
> *What a* + adjective + noun
> is a way to make a comment,
> like *What a busy day!* or
> *What a great lunch!*

B Check your answers.

C Practice the conversation
with a partner.
Use your own information.

Work In Pairs ⟨Student A⟩

Student B: Use page 132

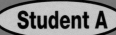

(A) Imagine a friend asked you to buy some groceries, but you weren't able to. Which of these do you think would be good excuses? Check (✔) them. Then compare your choices with your partner's.

1. _____ I forgot.
2. _____ I was too tired.
3. _____ I had to work overtime.

4. _____ I had to get my watch fixed.
5. _____ I went to see a movie instead.
6. _____ I ran into some friends.

(B) Ask questions and circle the errands your partner did.

• get a haircut
• go to art class
• pick up TV from repair shop
• pay rent

(C) Look at your schedule and answer your partner's questions. Give excuses where necessary.

Were you able to clean your room today?

SCHEDULE

7:00	go to the health club
8:00	
9:00	~~send package~~ → go to doctor's
10:00	
11:00	
12:00	
1:00	go to dentist
2:00	
3:00	
4:00	
5:00	
6:00	~~pick up photos~~ → pick up friend at airport
7:00	

Try this

Turn to page 132. Try the exercise again, but make up your own excuses.

Work In Pairs Student B

A Imagine a friend asked you to buy some groceries, but you weren't able to. Which of these do you think would be good excuses? Check (✔) them. Then compare your choices with your partner's.

1. _____ I forgot.
2. _____ I was too tired.
3. _____ I had to work overtime.

4. _____ I had to get my watch fixed.
5. _____ I went to see a movie instead.
6. _____ I ran into some friends.

B Look at your schedule and answer your partner's questions. Give excuses where necessary.

SCHEDULE

7:00	
8:00	
9:00	
10:00	
11:00	pay rent ⟶ take car to garage
12:00	
1:00	
2:00	
3:00	get haircut ⟶ meeting
4:00	
5:00	pick up TV from repair shop
6:00	
7:00	go to art class

C Ask questions and circle the errands your partner did.

- pick up photos
- go to dentist
- send package
- go to health club

Were you able to clean your room today?

Try this

Turn to page 131. Try the exercise again, but make up your own excuses.

8 Express Yourself

(A) Add two activities to the list.

Find someone who didn't...	Name	Reason
study English last night	_____	_____
eat breakfast this morning	_____	_____
clean his/her house yesterday	_____	_____
go out last weekend	_____	_____
bring his/her dictionary to class today	_____	_____
_____	_____	_____
_____	_____	_____

 Group work

(B) Survey your classmates. Write each person's name and their reason.

> I can't remember what this string is for.

9 Think About It

Many people have different ways to remember things. Some have electronic planners. Some make lists in a diary. Some leave messages on their home answering machines. Some tie strings around their fingers.

• *How about you? What do you do when you want to remember something?*

10 Write About It

(A) Look at the apology note.

> Dear Mom,
>
> Just a note to say I'm sorry for not getting Sally a birthday gift.
> I was going to do it this afternoon, but my computer crashed,
> and I had to take it to the repair shop.
>
> Jonathan

(B) Write a note to your teacher apologizing for not doing your English homework.

• *Strategy: Scanning*

Advice from Aunt Aggie

Dear Aunt Aggie,

I have a problem and I need you to give me some advice. I have been engaged to a woman for seven years. We are both 25. I think it is the right time to get married. So do my parents. However, my girlfriend keeps making excuses.

She says we're still too young; that we have to work hard and make money for our future; that we are not ready for such an important development in life. I disagree— we should marry now before we get any older. She says her career is important and wants to wait a few years. I think she is making excuses, and being unfair to me.

My parents have agreed to let us live with them after we marry. This way we could save money until we're ready to buy our own house. My girlfriend says "no." She says that couples should have their own place. I think this is just another excuse. What do you think?

I love her and want to settle down and raise a family. What should I do? Please help me.

Yours,
Heartbroken
Smithville, Ohio

Write the correct paragraph number in the spaces. Which paragraph talks about...

1. having children? ___4___

2. the couple's ages? _____

3. his girlfriend's job? _____

4. the length of their engagement? _____

5. his parents' opinion? _____

6. buying somewhere to live? _____

Talk About It

○ What advice should Aunt Aggie give, do you think?

○ Do you sometimes make excuses? In what situations?

○ Do you think making excuses is like lying? Why or why not? Give some examples.

1 Vocabulary Review

A Fill in the blanks with the correct places.

Where do you...

get your car fixed?	**Place**
get your eyes checked?	garage
get your teeth checked?	
get your shirts cleaned?	
get your watch fixed?	

B How often do you do the things on the list?

Did you do your homework last night?

No, I didn't. I was too busy.

2 Grammar Review

A Write questions using the words shown.

1. (return/videos)   Were you able to return the videos?
2. (pick/medicine) _____
3. (take/film/in) _____
4. (get/groceries) _____
5. (buy/milk) _____

B Imagine that the answer to the five questions above is *no*. Write an excuse for each.

1. _____
2. _____
3. _____
4. _____
5. _____

3 Log On

Practice more with the language and topics you studied on the *Expressions* website:

http://expressions.heinle.com

UNIT 1 *Language Summary* — *Can I have your name, please?*

What's your name? Can you tell me your name, please? Could/May I have your name, please?	It's Philip Hall.

What's your address? Can I have your address, please? Where do you live?	1013 Main Street.

What's your telephone number? Can you give me your phone number, please?	It's 711-2983.

I want to join the swimming club. I'd like to join the drama club, please.	Sure.

○ WORD BUILDER
Write down any new words from this unit you want to remember.

UNIT 2 *Language Summary* — *I have two older sisters.*

How many brothers and sisters do you have?	I have three. I have two older sisters and a younger brother. None. I'm an only child. I don't have any.
How many people are there in your family?	Five. There are five.

Do you all live together?	Yes, we do. No, my older sister lives in England.

○ WORD BUILDER
Write down any new words from this unit you want to remember.

UNIT 3 *Language Summary* *What are you doing over the break?*

What are you doing over the break?	I'm going to Paris.
How long are you staying there?	Five days.
	For a week.

What are you going to do over the break?	I'm going to take a computer class.
How long is the course?	Four weeks.
Where is it?	At the Cultural Center.

| Are you doing anything this weekend? | Yes, I'm visiting some relatives. |
| Are you going to do anything this weekend? | No, I'm going to stay home and watch TV. |

○ **WORD BUILDER**
Write down any new words from this unit you want to remember.

UNIT 4 *Language Summary* *Where did you go on vacation?*

| Where did you go on vacation? | I went to Chicago. |
| When did you get back? | Yesterday. |

Did you go anywhere last weekend?	Yes, I went to the beach.
What did you do there?	We went swimming.
Who did you go with?	With my family.
	My sister.

Did you have a good time?	Yeah, it was great.
Did you have fun?	I had a great time.
	It was OK.
	No, I didn't.

○ **WORD BUILDER**
Write down any new words from this unit you want to remember.

Language Summaries

Can I help you?	Yes, can I have a pack of cookies?
May I help you?	May I have a bottle of ketchup?
	A kilo of potatoes, please.
	I'll have a jar of salsa, please.

How much is this newspaper?	It's $.75.
How much are those postcards?	They're $.50 each.
How much is that?	That comes to $4.25 all together.

Anything else for you today?	No, that's all.
	Yes, I'll take a can of tuna, too.
Is that all?	Yes, that's all.
Will that be all for you?	Yes, that's it.

○ **WORD BUILDER**
Write down any new words from this unit you want to remember.

What do you do?	I'm an engineer.
	I sell computers.
Where do you work?	I work for Coretell Industries.
	Our office is in Baltimore.

Do you like your job?	It's great. I like working in an office.
Do you like it?	It's OK, but I don't like traveling very much.
What's your job like?	It's pretty interesting. I get to meet a lot of people.
What's it like?	Not so great. I don't get to travel a lot.

○ **WORD BUILDER**
Write down any new words from this unit you want to remember.

UNIT 7 *Language Summary* — *Could you do me a favor?*

Do you need some help? Can I help you?	Thanks. That would be great.
Do you need to type your report?	Yes. Could you give me a hand?

I need a copy of this document.	No problem.
I need to see Mr. Clark.	Fine. I'll call him for you.

Could you do me a favor? Could you do something for me? Could you help me make some copies?	OK, sure. No problem. Sorry, I'm busy right now.

Thanks./Thanks a lot./Thank you./ Thank you very much.	Sure. You're welcome. No problem. Don't mention it.

WORD BUILDER
Write down any new words from this unit you want to remember.

UNIT 8 *Language Summary* — *Are you looking forward to your trip?*

Do I have to make a reservation?	Yes, you do. No, you don't. You don't have to, but you should.

Should I take my laptop on vacation?	Yes, you should. You might want to check email. No, you shouldn't. Just relax and have a good time.

Are there any flights to Boston tomorrow?	Yes, there are. No, there aren't.
Do you have any buses to Chicago tonight? Do you have any rooms available for tonight?	Yes, we do. I'm sorry, we're fully booked.

I'd like to make a reservation, please. Can I reserve a seat on the 9:30 bus?	Sure. Can I have your name, please?

WORD BUILDER
Write down any new words from this unit you want to remember.

Can I help you,	sir? ma'am?	Yes, thank you. I need to cash a check.

I'm looking for a post office. Can you tell me how to get to the post office? Do you know where the post office is? How do I get to the post office?

Go straight Walk straight	on this street. up/down this street.
Turn left/right	at the gas station. at the corner of Wilson Ave. and Denver St. on Denver St.
You'll see it It's there	on the left. on your right.

○ **WORD BUILDER**
Write down any new words from this unit you want to remember.

I drink too much soda.
I think I eat too many cakes.
I don't exercise enough.
I want to play the piano better.

How much soda	do you drink?	Five cans a day.	That's a lot.
How many cakes	do you eat?	One a day.	That's too much.
How often	do you exercise?	Once a week.	That's too many.
	do you practice?	Once a month.	That's not enough.

○ **WORD BUILDER**
Write down any new words from this unit you want to remember.

Did you hear about Laura?

Did you hear about Jill?	No. What happened?

She	got	promoted. engaged. married. a new job. accepted to Harvard. her book published. a pay raise. her MBA.	Really? Are you kidding? Wow! That's great!
	won	a trip to Rome.	
	passed	her driver's test.	

Congratulations!	Thanks a lot.

○ WORD BUILDER

Write down any new words from this unit you want to remember.

I have a terrible headache.

What's the matter? What's wrong?	I don't feel well. I have a headache/a fever/ a cough/a sore throat.	You should see a doctor. I think you should take some aspirin. Go home and sleep.

How are you feeling now?	I feel better now, thanks. I feel much better now.
Is your headache gone?	Yes, I feel a lot better now. Yes, it is. Thank you.

○ WORD BUILDER

Write down any new words from this unit you want to remember.

UNIT 13 *Language Summary* — *Do you have any experience?*

Do you have any experience?	Yes, I worked as a sales manager for four years.
	Yes, I worked in a bookstore for two years.

What did you study at school?	I studied marketing.
What did you major in at university?	I majored in art.

Who's the best person for the job?	Joe has some experience.
	Jenny has more experience than Joe.
	Stella has the most experience in the group.
	Joe's a good person for the job.
	Jenny's a better person for the job.
	Stella is the best person for the job.

○ WORD BUILDER
Write down any new words from this unit you want to remember.

UNIT 14 *Language Summary* — *Have you been to the new mall?*

Are you doing anything this weekend?	Yes, I already have plans.
	No, I'm free.

Have you ever been to the zoo?	Yes, I have. It's kind of boring.
Have you been to the new coffee shop?	Yes, I've already been there.
	No, I haven't.
	No, not yet.
	No, I've never been there.

Do you want to go to a concert?	All right.
Would you like to go to the zoo?	That sounds good to me.

○ WORD BUILDER
Write down any new words from this unit you want to remember.

UNIT 15 Language Summary *I took your advice.*

I'm thinking about taking tennis lessons.	You should try La Vista Country Club. They have great instructors.

Why should we go to Hawaii?	Because it's nice and warm there.
Why should I go to the Virtual Institute?	Because you can learn about the Internet.
Why should Jenny buy a Land Cruiser?	Because they're safe, and they run great.

So, how was it?	It was wonderful.	Great. Glad to hear it.
How did it go?	They were really helpful.	I knew you would like them.
What did you think?	I'm glad I went.	I knew you would love it.
	I had a great time.	I knew you would have a good time.

⭕ WORD BUILDER
Write down any new words from this unit you want to remember.

UNIT 16 Language Summary *Did you mail those letters?*

Did you get the groceries?	Yes, I did. No, I didn't. I'll do it tomorrow. No, I wasn't able to.
Were you able to wash the car?	Yes, I washed it this morning. No, I wasn't.

Sorry.	I forgot.	That's OK.
I'm sorry.	I had to take the car to the garage.	
I'm really sorry.	I had to go to a meeting.	
	I didn't have time.	
	I had to get my watch fixed.	
	I had to get a hair cut.	

⭕ WORD BUILDER
Write down any new words from this unit you want to remember.

Congratulations! *You've finished Book 2.*

A) What did you enjoy about *Expressions*?

⬤ Check (✔) the boxes.

	Not at all	A little	A lot
I enjoyed the speaking activities.			
I enjoyed the listening activities.			
I enjoyed the reading activities.			
I enjoyed the writing activities.			
I enjoyed the grammar activities.			
I enjoyed the vocabulary activities.			
I am now a better English learner.			

B) Preferences

⬤ Which were the most useful for improving your English? Put them in order (1–6).

_____ Working on my own   _____ Role plays

_____ Pair work   _____ Review activities

_____ Group work   _____ Internet activities

C) Assess

⬤ Now look back at the chart on page 7. Are any of your choices different now? How?

⬤ How will you continue to improve your English? Write down four ideas.

○ _____
○ _____
○ _____
○ _____
○ _____
○ _____

Good luck with your continued English studies!